Surrey

Walks

Compiled by
Deborah King

Acknowledgements

I would like to thank Peter Cooper for accompanying me on many of these walks, and helping with photographs, Gill Gelatly for lending me some useful booklets, Surrey County Council, and all those responsible for maintaining the footpaths, bridleways and trails in the area.

Text:	Deborah King
Photography:	All by Deborah King and Peter Cooper, except p.52 and p.64 by Nick Channer
Editorial:	Ark Creative (UK) Ltd
Design:	Ark Creative (UK) Ltd

This product includes mapping data licensed from Ordnance Survey® with the permission of the Controller of Her Majesty's Stationery Office. © Crown Copyright 2010. All rights reserved. Licence number 150002047. Ordnance Survey, the OS symbol and Pathfinder are registered trademarks and Explorer, Landranger and Outdoor Leisure are trademarks of the Ordnance Survey, the national mapping agency of Great Britain.

ISBN: 978-1-85458-506-6

While every care has been taken to the publishers cannot accept respo changes in details given. The coun be removed, field boundaries can a in ownership can result in the clos paths. Also, paths that are easy and may become slippery, muddy and d stones across rivers and streams ma

If you find an inaccuracy in eithe the text or maps, please write to Crimson Publishing at the address below.

Printed in Singapore. 1/10

First published in Great Britain 2010 by Crimson Publishing, a division of:
Crimson Business Ltd,
Westminster House, Kew Road, Richmond, Surrey, TW9 2ND

www.totalwalking.co.uk

Front cover: View across to Westcott from Logmore Green
Previous page: Leith Hill Tower

Contents

Walking Safety; The Ramblers' Association; Walkers and the Law; Countryside Access Charter; Useful Organisations; Ordnance Survey Maps

Contents

Approximate walk times

Up to 2½ hours
Short walks on generally clear paths

2½–3½ hours
Slightly harder walks of moderate length

4 hours and over
Longer walks including some steep ascents/descents, occasionally on faint paths

The walk times are provided as a guide only and are calculated using an average walking speed of 2½mph (4km/h), adding one minute for each 10m (33ft) of ascent, and then rounding the result to the nearest half hour.

Walks are considered to be dog friendly unless specified.

At-a-glance

Walk	Page	Start	Nat. Grid Reference	Distance	Time	Height Gain
Albury Downs and St Martha's Hill	63	Newlands Corner	TQ 043492	7 miles (11.2km)	3½ hrs	985ft (300m)
Albury Park	26	Silent Pool car park, near Albury	TQ 059484	4½ miles (7.2km)	2 hrs	425ft (130m)
Box Hill	88	Box Hill	TQ 179513	11 miles (17.7km)	5½ hrs	1,720ft (525m)
Bramley and Farley Hill	48	Bramley	TQ 009447	6½ miles (10.4km)	3 hrs	490ft (150m)
Capel	16	Capel	TQ 176409	4 miles (6.4km)	2 hrs	130ft (40m)
Charlwood	24	Charlwood	TQ 241411	4¼ miles (6.8km)	2 hrs	230ft (70m)
Chobham Common	33	Staple Hill car park	SU 972647	5¼ miles (8.4km)	2½ hrs	165ft (50m)
Churt Valley	30	Churt	SU 854385	5 miles (8km)	2½ hrs	525ft (160m)
Compton and Loseley Park	42	Compton	SU 956474	6 miles (9.6km)	3 hrs	445ft (135m)
Cranleigh	28	Knowle Lane, Cranleigh	TQ 059388	5 miles (8km)	2 hrs	150ft (45m)
The Devil's Punchbowl	36	Hindhead	SU 890357	5¼ miles (8.4km)	2½ hrs	605ft (185m)
Effingham Forest and Netley Heath	80	West Hanger car park	TQ 070493	9½ miles (15.2km)	4½ hrs	820ft (250m)
Farley Heath	45	Farley Heath	TQ 052448	6 miles (9.6km)	3 hrs	575ft (175m)
Frensham Common	73	Frensham Little Pond	SU 856418	7¾ miles (12.5km)	3½ hrs	360ft (110m)
Godstone	18	Godstone	TQ 350515	4 miles (6.4km)	2 hrs	260ft (80m)
Gomshall and the Abingers	77	Gomshall	TQ 088478	8 miles (13km)	4 hrs	755ft (230m)
Leigh	22	Leigh	TQ 224470	4 miles (6.4km)	2 hrs	n/a
Leith Hill and Friday Street	51	Car park near Coldharbour village	TQ 147432	6½ miles (10.5km)	3 hrs	900ft (275m)
Limpsfield	57	Ridlands Lane, Limpsfield	TQ 418522	7 miles (11.2km)	3½ hrs	590ft (180m)
Outwood and its Mill	70	Outwood	TQ 326456	7½ miles (12km)	3½ hrs	345ft (105m)
Puttenham Common	12	Suffield Lane, Puttenham	SU 920462	2¾ miles (4.4km)	1½ hrs	330ft (100m)
Reigate and Colley Hills	14	Reigate Hill	TQ 262523	3¾ miles (6km)	2 hrs	540ft (165m)
Ripley Green and the River Wey	54	Ripley Green	TQ 053569	7 miles (11.2km)	3 hrs	n/a
Shabden and Upper Gatton Park	60	Elmore Pond, Chipstead	TQ 278568	7 miles (11.2km)	3½ hrs	770ft (235m)
Shere and Hurt Wood	84	Winterfold Heath	TQ 074425	9½ miles (15.2km)	4½ hrs	985ft (300m)
Tilford and Waverley	39	Tilford	SU 873434	5¾ miles (9.2km)	3 hrs	575ft (175m)
Westcott	20	Westcott	TQ 141486	4 miles (6.4km)	2 hrs	540ft (165m)
Witley to Haslemere via Chiddingfold	66	Witley Station	SU 948379	7¼ miles (11.6km)	3½ hrs	490ft (150m)

Comments

Both at the start of the walk on the Albury Downs and from St Martha's Church, the highest points on the walk, there are superb views over the North Downs and Weald.

This walk traces the history of Albury including the ancient church where the village once stood, its new church when the village relocated, and delightful scenery including the eerie Silent Pool.

The walk opens with the spectacular view from Box Hill, yet there is no anticlimax in what follows. There are steep gradients, and the way can be muddy so allow adequate time and take refreshments.

This invigorating walk offers sweeping views from the top of Farley Hill and includes some shady bridleways. Can be prone to mud after heavy rain.

Mainly across farmland this easy walk begins and ends in the lovely village of Capel. There is a 12th century church to explore.

An 11th century church, a lovely stretch of woodland and some tranquil paths give this walk a rural feel in spite of its proximity to Gatwick Airport.

Rich in wildlife and fungi this lovely walk highlights the varied habitats of Chobham Common. There is also a prehistoric earthwork on the route.

This walk passes through conifer plantations and heathland of bracken and fern. Churt village has an ancient pub and a mammoth tusk and bones were also found nearby.

There are three highlights to this walk: Watts Cemetery Chapel, Loseley House and St Nicholas Church in Compton. The walk also includes a good stretch of the North Downs Way.

The route has no taxing gradient as it winds through meadows to a disused canal towpath. The final section is also level, following an abandoned railway, The Downs Link.

This upland walk follows the rim of the Devil's Punchbowl. The outward part is through woodland, and the return climbs to sandy heathland and the summit of Gibbet Hill.

There is much to see on this long, scenic walk including pillboxes, Netley Heath and its link with the Second World War, historic Troy Bridge, and an area of rare chalk grassland.

There is lots of attractive scenery along this route and the chance to visit the remains of Farley Roman Temple.

The pines of Frensham Common contribute to a landscape that could belong to Scotland, while in contrast the ridge of Kettlebury Hill provides excellent walking with views extending over Surrey.

Part of the walk is along the Greensand Way and apart from the attractive scenery, there is also plenty to see, including the tombstone of an avid rambler whose works saved many of our footpaths.

Train spotters will find this walk of interest as the route follows the railway for some of the time, but trains are infrequent. The route passes a secluded church at Wotton which is well worth a visit.

An undemanding, level walk and unusually for Surrey, one that is fairly open with no woodland tracks. There are some fine views over to the North Downs and a lovely church to explore at the start.

A woodland and heathland walk that climbs to the highest point in south east England, a magnificent vantage point over the Weald.

This walk in eastern Surrey close to the Kent border highlights the distinctive woodland in this area fed by chalk springs and the small sections of heathland, such as Limpsfield Common.

You'll see plenty of hedgerow restoration on this walk and Outwood Windmill is Britain's oldest working windmill.

There are some interesting highlights including General's Pond, Iron-Age Hillbury fort and a glimpse of a house built by Edwin Lutyens, the well-known local architect.

The first half of this well-wooded walk is along the ridge of the North Downs; the second half follows the Pilgrims' Way along the base of that ridge.

A scenic route including a mill, three locks and a pleasant section of walking along the River Wey.

An easy to follow, well-waymarked route with good views of rolling hills and parkland with livestock grazing. Plenty of mixed woodlands and farmland and plenty of stiles.

Highlights of this rewarding walk include the villages of Peaslake and Shere as well as the climb to the top of Pitch Hill. The route also passes through Hurt Wood and Winterfold Forest.

Take a picnic on this walk – the village green has cricket in summer and Waverley Abbey's setting beside the River Wey is idyllic.

The undulating route follows an attractive section of the Greensand Way before returning via Westcott Heath along a sheltered byway.

This linear walk in the Low Weald includes the delightful village of Chiddingfold, beautiful areas of rolling hills, the town of Haslemere and a short train journey back to the start.

Introduction
to Surrey

Surrey is easily within reach of London but despite its commuter belt image and proximity to the M25 and Gatwick and Heathrow airports there is a surprising amount of unspoilt and rich countryside in the county.

This is an attractive area for walkers as the terrain is varied, ranging from the open ridge tops of the North Downs that offer extensive views to the slopes of the greensand ridge and the ubiquitous forests. Today, Surrey has some of the most extensive tree cover of any county in England. It also has some of the densest networks of public footpaths and bridleways in the country, supplemented by country parks and the large areas maintained by the National Trust. There can be no other part of England that is criss-crossed by more long distance and recreational paths including the national trails of the North Downs Way, the Greensand Way, Pilgrim's Way, Vanguard Way and the Downs Link not to mention the many locally named trails including the Fox Way, a 39-mile circuit of walks in the Guildford area, and the Serpent Trail.

One of the best ways to explore the county is on foot; often in the footsteps of pilgrims and drovers, to see a rural landscape that has hardly altered: small, pretty villages of Saxon and medieval origin, chalk slopes with isolated farmsteads, large country houses with enormous parklands, remnants of pre-Industrial Revolution industry, the ruins of ancient abbeys and a plethora of meandering streams, and waterways to name but a few.

One of the main geographical features is the North Downs Way, a 153-mile trail stretching from Farnham in the west of Surrey past Reigate in the east, much of which follows the Pilgrim's Way, a historic route used by those making pilgrimages to pray at holy shrines. The Greensand Way is another long distance trail and stretches for 108 miles passing the Devil's Punch Bowl, Winterfold Heath and Pitch and Leith Hills before continuing into Kent. Below the downs lies the Weald, a complex and scenically varied area of sandstone and clay, once covered by the vast ancient forest of Andredesweald. A few miles south of the North Downs the heavily wooded greensand ridge rises to 965 feet (294m) at Leith hill, the highest point in south east England. For an area lying between London, Kent and Sussex it is hard to imagine that this was once wild and remote. Weald means 'wild' and the region was largely cut off from the rest of the country by thick forest and rough heath.

Today, heathland is one of the most threatened habitats in Europe and more than three quarters of that in England has been lost since 1800. The remaining 20 per cent of lowland heath left in Surrey is found mainly in the north west and the south west of the county and is now protected.

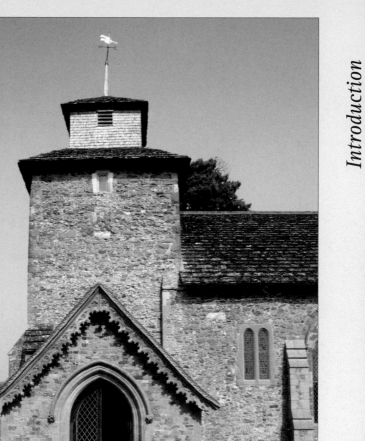

The church at Wotton

A particularly beautiful area is The Surrey Hills, a band of unspoilt woodland valleys and heath, which in 1958 was one of the first landscapes to be designated an Area of Outstanding Natural Beauty (AONB). It stretches across a quarter of the county to include the chalk slopes of the North Downs from Farnham in the west, Oxted in the east and extends south to the Greensand Hills that rise from Haslemere, and Limpsfield. The area is characterised by sloping wooded ridges overlooking the valleys to the north and is rich in grassland flowers, ancient woodlands and wildlife and offers some of the best walking in southern England. With almost 40 per cent coverage it is also one of the most wooded of the AONBs.

Almost one quarter of Surrey itself is wooded – well above the national

Churt village sign

average – making it Britain's most wooded county – a fact endorsed by Surrey's official logo of two interlocking oak leaves. Much of this is mature woodland and most of its many beauty spots are highlighted in the pages that follow, notably Box Hill, which has the oldest untouched area of natural woodland in the UK and is located on a prominent chalk escarpment overlooking the River Mole; Leith Hill, which is the highest point in southern England; Puttenham and Crooksbury Commons; the dramatic heather-clad basin of the Devil's Punch Bowl at Hindhead; Frensham Common and Frensham Little Pond, a 13th century man-made pond alongside a fine example of open heathland and one of the many areas in Surrey designated a Site of Special Scientific Interest (SSSI); and Chobham Common, one of the best remaining examples of lowland heath.

The walks also incorporate views of some attractive and historic houses such as the Regency villa of Polesden Lacey, Loseley House, the rolling parkland of Shabden and Upper Gatton Park and the grand remains of others including Waverley Abbey and Newark Priory, as well as Britain's oldest working windmill.

Surrey has some interesting historic churches such as the Saxon church in Albury Park, the isolated church in Wotton, St Martha's near Newland's Corner and Compton's 10th century St Nicholas church. On the walks you will also see some remarkable architecture such as Watt's Cemetery and its stunning and unique chapel influenced by the Arts & Crafts Movement, buildings designed by Edwin Lutyens and gardens by Gertrude Jekyll.

Many idyllic villages can be found along the routes. Shere, which has some very old properties and the River Tilling Bourne flowing through it, is often used for filming, as is nearby Peaslake. Chiddingfold is another attractive village with a pub, duck pond and church beside its village green.

The Romans built a road to link Surrey with the south coast via London to their headquarters in Colchester and parts of this road, Stane Street, have been incorporated into our current roads system but walkers are also likely to come across it as some sections survive as footpaths. Although relatively few artefacts from the Roman period have been found in Surrey the site of a Roman Temple near Farley Green and a number of hill forts and earthworks can be seen on some of the walks in this book.

From around AD480 Saxons from the south and Jutes from the east invaded and began to settle in the area and establish a sub-kingdom. At this time the Surrey area was sparsely populated and almost entirely forested. Farming practices over the years have created an assorted landscape of fields, hedgerows and copses all of which result in an excellent terrain for walking.

It was the railways and later the roads, that brought about the greatest transformation of all, making it possible for much of the region to become a desirable commuter area for people working in London. The heyday of the Wealden iron industry during the 16th and 17th centuries, along with improved farming techniques, brought wealth to the area and many of the fine manor houses and farms were built at this time. As charcoal was used in the smelting of iron, it was the iron industry that was responsible for the destruction of much of the Weald's extensive forest. By the 18th century an increasing shortage of timber, plus the development of coke using coal to replace the charcoal smelting, caused the industry to move northwards to the coalfields of the Midlands. This meant the remaining woodlands were saved and the area spared the environmental consequences of the Industrial Revolution. Remnants of this era are evident today and a couple of the walks pass hammer ponds, which were formed by damming the stream at various points along its course, and the watermills which operated the heavy hammers of the iron works. At Abinger Hammer for, example, these ponds are still known as hammer ponds but nowadays the chalk beds have been found ideal for the growing of watercress. Another walk that passes a hammer pond is Leith Hill near Friday Street and it's hard to imagine how this quiet area must once have been so busy with the noisy clatter of activity. Surrey now has more millionaires than anywhere else in the country and it has been transformed from a poor, backwater into a busy, prosperous county. Luckily for walkers there is a wealth of footpaths and bridleways to explore off the beaten track in some of the loveliest parts of our country.

This book includes a list of waypoints alongside the description of the walk, so that you can enjoy the full benefits of gps should you wish to. For more information on using your gps, read the *Pathfinder® Guide GPS for Walkers,* by gps teacher and navigation trainer, Clive Thomas (ISBN 978-0-7117-4445-5). For essential information on map reading and basic navigation, read the *Pathfinder® Guide Map Reading Skills* by outdoor writer, Terry Marsh (ISBN 978-0-7117-4978-8). Both titles are available in bookshops or can be ordered online at www.totalwalking.co.uk

Puttenham Common

Start	Puttenham Common, off Suffield Lane	**GPS waypoints**
Distance	2¾ miles (4.4km)	☑ SU 920 462
Height gain	330 feet (100m)	Ⓐ SU 917 460
Approximate time	1½ hours	Ⓑ SU 910 462
		Ⓒ SU 911 473
Parking	Car park off Suffield Lane	Ⓓ SU 917 473
Route terrain	Grassy, heathland paths and sandy bridleways	
Ordnance Survey maps	Landranger 186 (Aldershot & Guildford), Explorer 145 (Guildford & Farnham)	

This short walk is a perfect example of a lowland heathland area and the plants and trees that grow in this type of environment. It crosses Puttenham Common and continues uphill past an Iron Age hillfort before returning along a short stretch of the North Downs Way. There are also some fine views over towards the Hog's Back and the Devil's Punchbowl.

☑ With your back to the car park entrance off Suffield Lane, take the grassy path on the left heading downhill towards trees. At a path junction turn left into Suffield Lane, turn right and after 40 yds turn right again at a bridleway sign Ⓐ.

Keep ahead at a wide path crossing along the narrow bridleway and follow

Crossing of paths on Puttenham Common

this path as it crosses a series of bridleways and footpaths all the way to General's Pond, named after General James Oglethorpe who bought the Puttenham estate in 1744 but lived mostly in Godalming. Oglethorpe was a philanthropist and prison reformer who founded the American colony of Georgia and sailed with the first 115 settlers from Gravesend in 1722.

Turn right at a bridleway sign to skirt the pond Ⓑ, and at a fork by a fingerpost, bear right uphill to arrive at a sandy path junction. Bear left and then immediately right at a purple waymarker. On your left are the remains of the Iron-Age Hillbury fort, most likely built for defensive purposes

and from where there are good views of the Hog's Back to the north and the hills surrounding the Devil's Punchbowl to the south. Archaeologists have discovered flints, ashes and sections of bone from the area relating to every period except Saxon. Notice the landscape here – this area has low rainfall and due to the lack of calcium in the soil and its inability to hold water and nutrients, hilltops like this are the driest.

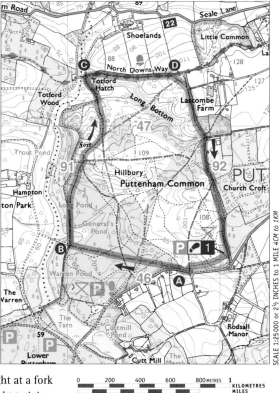

SCALE 1:25000 or 2½ INCHES to 1 MILE 4CM to 1KM

Head downhill to a crossing of paths and turn left following the purple waymarker. Bear right at a fork and at a T-junction turn right to join the North Downs Way **G**.

| 0 | 200 | 400 | 600 | 800 METRES | 1 | |
| 0 | 200 | 400 | 600 YARDS | ½ | | KILOMETRES MILES |

Many Neolithic flints have been found on the borders of the parish north of this section of the walk. At a North Downs Way waymarked fingerpost, turn right through a set of wooden posts on to a grassy, heathland path **D** that passes Lascombe House. This house was built in the 1890s by Edwin Lutyens who was raised in Surrey and after training as an architect in London, returned to design many more buildings in the county. For the design of Lascombe he collaborated, as he often did, with the well-known garden designer, Gertrude Jekyll, whom he had been introduced to a few years earlier. Jekyll, who is now considered to be one of the greatest of all English garden designers, spent most of her time in Surrey and wrote thousands of articles for gardening magazines. She was greatly influenced

by the Arts & Crafts Movement and would explore the landscape and architecture of south west Surrey with Lutyens in her pony cart.

Continue along the bridleway through trees, by a wooden fence on your left, along the edge of Puttenham Common, which was once part of a much larger area of heathland and is now a Site of Special Scientific Interest. You'll see heathland shrubs like bell heather and gorse in the more open areas and many silver birch, oak and Scots Pine trees as well as the ubiquitous bracken, which offers some wonderful hues whatever the season and is one of the few plants that can survive in lower heathland like this one.

Finally, bear right at a fingerpost to cross the common and return to the car park. ●

Reigate and Colley Hills

		GPS waypoints
Start	Reigate Hill, off Wray Lane	
Distance	3¾ miles (6km)	☑ TQ 262 523
Height gain	540 feet (165m)	Ⓐ TQ 250 520
Approximate time	2 hours	Ⓑ TQ 238 523
Parking	Car park off Wray Lane	Ⓒ TQ 239 520
Route terrain	Stoney tracks, woodland paths and one steep ascent	Ⓓ TQ 256 517
Ordnance Survey maps	Landranger 187 (Dorking & Reigate), Explorer 146 (Dorking, Boxhill and Reigate)	

This walk starts from the top of Reigate Hill and follows the ridge of the North Downs – well-wooded but with some grand views – across the adjacent Reigate and Colley Hills, both owned by the National Trust, before descending and then continuing along the base of them, following the Pilgrims' Way through woodland. The only part of the route that is quite strenuous comes near the end: a steep climb up a narrow path to regain the top of Reigate Hill.

📝 Begin by walking past the **refreshment kiosk** and toilets to cross the footbridge over the main road and continue along a wooded track, from which there are fine views to the left over Reigate and the neighbouring countryside. The chalk downland you are on is part of the Surrey Hills Area of Outstanding Natural Beauty and is a mixture of open grassland and woodland. On meeting a tarmac drive keep ahead along it – after the last house it becomes a rough track – and pass between Reigate Fort on the left and a water tower on the right, to enter the National Trust property of Reigate Hill.

Reigate Fort was built by the Victorians to defend London from a possible French invasion and its role was to supply tools and ammunition so that soldiers could dig entrenched positions along the North Downs. Continue along the beautifully wooded track (the Millennium Way), passing some fine old oak trees, to reach the circular, classical style pavilion on Colley Hill Ⓐ. This was originally built as a drinking fountain and bears the inscription: *'Presented to the Corporation of the Borough of Reigate for the Benefit of the Public by Lieutenant-Colonel Robert William Inglis in 1909'.*

This is a magnificent viewpoint, looking along the ridge of the North Downs to Box Hill and across to Leith Hill and the greensand ridge. A toposcope indicates the features that can be seen from here. Continue over Colley Hill, along the North Downs Way, still following a tree-lined track. Go through a gate just after a National Trust sign to Colley Hill and keep ahead by a fence on the left, and continue to a tarmac drive Ⓑ.

Turn left and then turn left again in

front of a gate and fence, along an enclosed path that heads steeply downhill; a gap in the trees reveals a superb view to the right over the Surrey countryside. The path curves to the right and continues down to a crossing of paths. Turn left here, **C**, through a wooden barrier with a yellow waymark, to leave the North Downs Way and join the Pilgrims' Way.

Colley Hill pavilion

Now keep along an attractive wooded path that winds and undulates along the base of first Colley and later Reigate Hill, initially passing some fine old yews. At a waymarked post turn right and at a fork, keep ahead along the right-hand path to go down steps, bear left at the bottom of them, go down a few more steps to a T-junction and then bear left. Continue along the base of Reigate Hill, curving right at one point, eventually passing beside a barrier and a National Trust Pilgrims' Way sign onto a tarmac lane.

Keep ahead for about 100 yds and where the lane bends to the right, bear left along a track at a bridleway sign,

initially between walls on both sides, still along the base of Reigate Hill. Continue between houses on the edge of Reigate to emerge onto the main road, turn left and after a few yards bear left, **D**, signposted 'Public Footpath' to follow a yellow waymarked path steeply uphill.

Near the top by a wooden fence on the right, after passing Rock Farm, the path broadens into a clear track which continues up to a tarmac drive by a bend. Turn right, at a Millennium Trail sign, along a track and retrace your steps to the start. ●

```
0        200    400    600    800 METRES   1
|__|__|__|__|__|__|__|__|__|__|_____  KILOMETRES
                                            MILES
0        200    400    600 YARDS    1/2
```

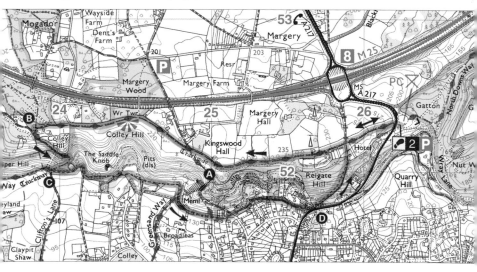

Capel

Start	At the Memorial Hall in The Street, Capel	
Distance	4 miles (6.4km)	
Height gain	130 feet (40m)	
Approximate time	2 hours	
Parking	At the Memorial Hall or by the church	
Route terrain	Cross-field and woodland paths	
Ordnance Survey maps	Landranger 187 (Dorking & Reigate), Explorer 146 (Dorking, Boxhill and Reigate)	

GPS waypoints

🖉 TQ 176 409
Ⓐ TQ 177 413
Ⓑ TQ 189 418
Ⓒ TQ 195 406
Ⓓ TQ 186 403

A pleasant, fairly level walk through the village of Capel in the Mole Valley passing some old farms. There are open views and this walk passes near to the site of a most unusual mill, which was mentioned by the Anglo-French writer Hilaire Belloc in one of his books.

🖉 With your back to the Memorial Hall in The Street, Capel, turn right along the road and just after it curves left, turn right at a public footpath sign, and climb a stile Ⓐ.

Follow the enclosed footpath and skirt round three sides of the field to cross a wooden footbridge with a stile at each end. Continue along the grassy path, go over another stile and then cross a bridleway, to join a road (Misbrooks Green Road). Where the road bends left keep ahead, at a public footpath sign beside Broomell's Farm. Go through a gate, cross a paddock, go over a stile and cross the field to enter woodland via a gate. Maintain your direction through the woodland and go over a stile to follow the field edge path to the left of Green's Copse. About 50 yds before the end of the field turn left across the field and go over a stile to the road where you turn right for a few yards and turn right along the track to

Greens Farm Ⓑ. The original settlement of Capel had around 30 farms and mixed farming was popular until the 17th century when brickyards began to appear. The heavy clay here was used to make the bricks and limekilns were constructed to make the binding: a mixture of lime, sand and water. One of these limekilns is next to the pond at Greens Farm and was first identified on an Ordnance Survey map in 1873.

Just past the farm, where a lane swings in from the left, turn right at a public footpath signpost. Pass between farm buildings and turn left in front of a pond. Go over a stile to the right of a hedge and keep along the left-hand field edge looking out for where you turn left to go over a stile. Bear right over a concrete footbridge then bear right along the field edge, go over a stile in the corner and then turn right along the bridleway Ⓒ.

Go through a gate, then over another

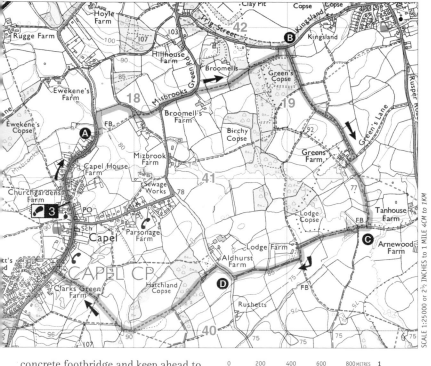

concrete footbridge and keep ahead to go through a hedge gap and follow the path along the right edge of a field to a waymarked post. Bear left and at a T-junction turn left for 100 yds. Go through a gate on the right to join another bridleway across a field and go through a gate onto a lane **Ⓓ**.

Turn right and after 100 yds turn left along a bridleway, bearing right at a fork to reach a three-way signpost on the edge of woodland. Keep ahead across the field and bear right to go over a stile and plank footbridge. Follow the path through a belt of trees and then as it curves right over another footbridge and continues gently uphill through a young plantation.

It was close to this point that Shiremark Mill once stood. The smock-type cornmill was built in 1774 and unusual for being the only type of its kind south of the Thames. Its 'hurst frame' design was more commonly found in watermills than windmills.

It was worked by wind until 1919 but despite being listed as an antiquity, it was regarded too expensive to repair and became derelict. The mill is mentioned in Hilaire Belloc's preface to his book *The Four Men*.

Continue along an enclosed path to arrive at a road. Turn right and continue past the village's 12th-century church and **The Crown** pub to the start of the walk.

Green's Copse woodland

Godstone

		GPS waypoints
Start	Village pond, Godstone	
Distance	4 miles (6.4km)	TQ 350 515
Height gain	260 feet (80m)	**A** TQ 357 515
		B TQ 360 510
Approximate time	2 hours	**C** TQ 371 512
Parking	Next to the village pond (3 hours	**D** TQ 372 507
	maximum stay)	**E** TQ 348 511
Route terrain	Bridleway, farmland footpaths	
Dog friendly	Keep on a lead through Godstone Farm	
Ordnance Survey maps	Landranger 187 (Dorking & Reigate), Explorer 146 (Dorking, Boxhill and Reigate)	

An easy walk that passes an historic nature reserve, once a site used in the making of gunpowder, and goes through some attractive farmland on the edge of Godstone. The latter half follows the Greensand Way. The Pond at Godstone Green was used as a horse pond in the 19th century and waggoners would drive their horses down its sloping bank.

From the pond cross the road, take the public footpath beside the **White Hart** pub in the direction of the church. Pass beside Bay Pond and its nature reserve, which was originally built to power the local gunpowder mill at nearby Leigh Mill, then cross the road ahead and follow the footpath to the right of St Nicholas churchyard.

This is a quiet area known as Church Town, and it has many old timber-framed buildings. Church End and Church House, both opposite the church are examples of buildings erected when brick became fashionable in the 18th century. As well as restoring the church Sir George Gilbert Scott also designed

The Greensand Way, near Godstone

the adjacent almshouses in a Gothic and Tudor style. There is a wonderful little chapel here too.

In the churchyard you can find the tombstone of Edmund Taylor, nicknamed Walker Miles who lived most of his life in Camberwell, south London but moved to Godstone shortly before his untimely death at the age of 54. He wrote 30 volumes called *Fieldpath Rambles* and his works are thought to have saved many of our public footpaths from neglect or destruction.

At the end of the churchyard pass between the wooden posts of a redundant gate **A**.

Follow the meandering path past Glebe Water, where kingfishers can sometimes be seen, and the path bends sharply to the right and then ascends a grassy verge on the left to a field. Head diagonally right across the field to join a woodland path and at a fork turn right along the right-hand field edge to a track where you turn left **B**.

Follow the bridleway under the A22 and when you reach the 17th century Hop Garden Cottage turn right and then keep ahead to Jackass Lane and turn right **C**.

At the top of the lane bear right down Tandridge Lane. Turn right at the public

footpath sign to join the Greensand Way **D**.

Follow this pleasant footpath between fields all the way to the A22. Go through a kissing-gate, cross the road and take the footpath opposite into woodland. Go through another kissing-gate and follow the Greensand Way waymarkers to go over a ford to a road. Turn right here to leave the Greensand Way. Just after a bus stop, turn left along Enterdent Road and after 50 yds turn right at the public footpath sign into woodland. The path ascends steeply to reach a stile. Climb this and follow the grassy path to climb another stile. The path runs alongside the adventure playground of Godstone Farm, popular with families, to a stile. Go over it, follow the path to the road, and turn right.

After 200 yds look out for where you turn left at a public footpath sign and continue along this enclosed path with backs of houses to your right and farmland to your left, to Ivy Mill Lane **E**.

Turn right and then right again at the village green to return to the start of the walk by the village pond.   ●

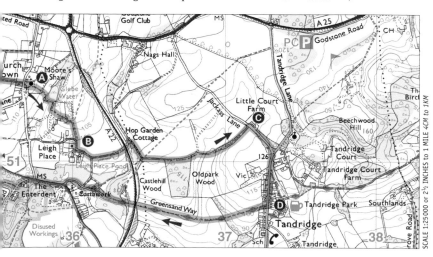

Westcott

		GPS waypoints
Start	Westcott	☑ TQ 141 486
Distance	4 miles (6.4km)	**Ⓐ** TQ 140 485
Height gain	540 feet (165m)	**Ⓑ** TQ 149 485
Approximate time	2 hours	**Ⓒ** TQ 150 481
Parking	By the village green in Westcott Street	**Ⓓ** TQ 137 466
		Ⓔ TQ 132 473
Route terrain	Bridleway, grassy paths, quiet lanes	
Ordnance Survey maps	Landranger 187 (Dorking & Reigate), Explorer 146 (Dorking, Boxhill and Reigate)	

A fairly easy and undulating walk from the village green in Westcott linking up with the Greensand Way for a while before leaving it to pass beside woodland and returning along a sheltered lane with some panoramic views of the valley and Westcott, which sits at the foot of the North Downs and the slopes of Leith Hill to the south.

🖎 From the village green cross the A25 and at **The Cricketers** pub turn left and after a few paces, turn left again at a public footpath sign **Ⓐ**.

Head uphill and at a public footpath sign for the Greensand Way, turn left and cross a tarmac drive by houses. Go through a kissing-gate and continue as this enclosed section of the Greensand Way climbs and then descends. Cross a wooden footbridge and at a gravel bridleway, turn right **Ⓑ**.

Go through a kissing-gate and follow the path along the edge of woodland to a waymarked post where you turn right and cross a plank footbridge **Ⓒ**.

The path passes to the right of two lakes – a mixed course fishery – next to Old Bury Hill House.

The Bury Hill estate was formed in the 18th century by Edward Walter who bought a farm to the south and the land nearby until he accumulated around

1,600 acres. In 1815 Bury Hill was sold off in lots and Robert Barclay purchased almost 1,000 acres. Apart from wealth Barclay also had a flair for gardening and he created the large, ornamental lakes. During the Second World War the house was occupied by the military and much of it is now privately owned apartments.

It was mainly due to the posterity of this house, and Rookery, which comes later in the walk, that enabled Westcott to grow into the village it is today. Although it's only 1½ miles west of Dorking and the main Guildford Road passes through it, Westcott was always associated with local agriculture until it expanded during the Victorian period. In 1852 Sir George Gilbert Scott who also designed the Albert Memorial in Hyde Park built the Holy Trinity Church.

Turn right, following waymarkers, over a stile and plank footbridge to

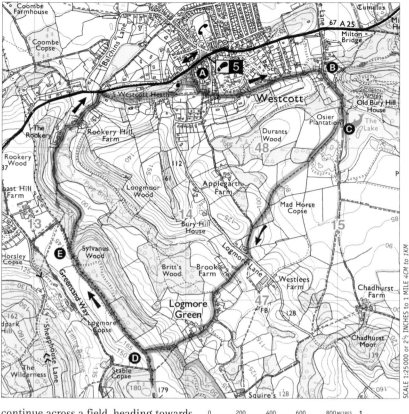

SCALE 1:25000 or 2½ INCHES to 1 MILE 4CM to 1KM

continue across a field, heading towards Mad Horse Copse. Climb a stile and follow the enclosed path beside a field, to climb another stile, and later, go through a kissing-gate at a path junction. Bear left to cross Logmore Lane and follow the bridleway opposite along a tarmac lane that eventually passes Logmore Farm. Go through a gate and along the narrow, enclosed bridleway that ascends to a T-junction with Wolvens Lane, a sheltered byway, and turn right **D**. This section of the walk runs parallel with the Greensand Way over to your left and to the right you may see the North Downs in the distance with the outskirts of Dorking in the middle distance.

After ½ mile, at a hedge gap, turn right at a three-way signpost **E**, to ascend along a bridleway which the Greensand Way later joins from the left.

After a row of houses turn right along a lane and follow it to a public footpath sign just before the Guildford Road (A25). Turn right here, still following the Greensand Way along an uphill section of tree roots for steps. At a tarmac drive, turn right and almost immediately turn left following Greensand Way waymarkers across Westcott Heath. Here you'll see a bench dedicated to those who died during an air raid in 1944. At the lane bear left, past Holy Trinity Church to the A25 and as you retrace your steps to the start, notice the thatched dovecot, which spells W.E.S.T, on the village green. The weathervane on top of the dovecot has quirkily had the N replaced by a T. ●

Leigh

		GPS waypoints
Start	St Bartholomew Church, Leigh	
Distance	4 miles (6.4km)	◢ TQ 224 470
Height gain	Negligible	Ⓐ TQ 214 470
		Ⓑ TQ 209 477
Approximate time	2 hours	Ⓒ TQ 210 486
Parking	Roadside parking opposite St Bartholomew Church	Ⓓ TQ 223 486
Route terrain	Stiles, grassy field paths and some lanes	
Dog friendly	Livestock grazing	
Ordnance Survey maps	Landranger 187 (Dorking & Reigate), Explorer 146 (Dorking, Boxhill and Reigate)	

This is an easy stroll across some open countryside. Leigh means a clearing in the woods and the route is surrounded by some lovely woodland and crosses a brook. The community here has always been self-sufficient and a sense of remoteness is evident on the walk, which also passes Leigh Place, a manor house dating from the 15th century.

📝 Facing the church turn right, past **The Plough** pub and at the road junction, turn right along Tapners Road. After 600 yds where the road swings to the right keep ahead along Bunce Common Road, passing **The Seven Stars** pub. Just after the cricket club look out for a public footpath sign on the right Ⓐ and climb the stile then cross the field to a waymarked post at the hedge gap where you climb a stile and cross a plank footbridge. Bear diagonally left across the next field to go through another hedge gap. Ahead there are some lovely views of the chalky escarpment of the North Downs.

Keep along the left-hand edge of the field and after climbing a stile in the far left corner the path becomes enclosed. Cross a wooden footbridge over Gad Brook and keep initially along the left edge of the next field, then follow the row of poplars to a road Ⓑ at the

driveway to Hall Farm.

Turn right and where the road curves right, turn left at a public footpath sign beside Gadbrook House. Follow the path between fields, go over a wooden footbridge over a ditch and continue along the next field beside a ditch on your left. Climb a stile, go over a plank footbridge to a road Ⓒ where you turn right.

After a short while turn right at a public footpath sign and hop over a stile to pass to the right of a plantation, and a house, to reach a road. Cross the road, climb the stile opposite and head for the top left-hand corner of the field to climb another two stiles.

Once over these follow the line of oak trees, past a wire fence on the right and cross the next field to where a public footpath sign directs you diagonally right along a cross-field path to a yellow waymarker.

Keep ahead beside a hedge on the

Footbridge over River Mole

right to a stile. Climb this and continue through a narrow belt of trees to a concrete bridge over the River Mole. Do not cross this bridge but turn right in front of it and climb an embankment to a three-way footpath junction **D**.

Turn left, following the hedge line and where it curves left, keep ahead across the field towards a copse. Climb the stile, cross the footbridge and bear half right across the field ahead, passing to the right of a large oak tree. Maintain this direction to go through a hedge gap

at a public footpath sign and then climb the stile and bear left diagonally across the field, now with a hedge on your right, to reach another stile beside a set of yellow waymarkers. Climb the stile and keep beside the hedge on the right across two fields, then continue along a track towards a farmhouse to a road.

Cross the road, climb the stile by a public footpath sign opposite and continue ahead to climb another stile and a plank footbridge.

Turn right and go through a hedge gap by a yellow waymarker then bear slightly left across the field. Leigh Place with its moat and medieval fishponds is over to the right. Go through a kissing-gate in the corner of the field and turn left along the road back to the church.●

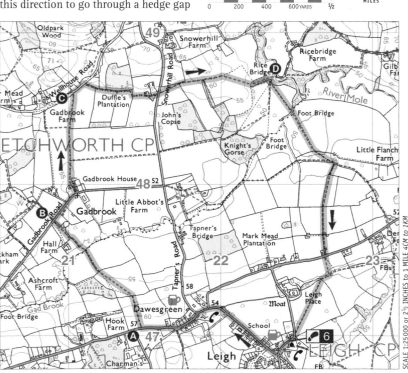

Charlwood

		GPS waypoints
Start	St Nicholas Church, The Street, Charlwood	TQ 241 411
Distance	4¼ miles (6.8km)	**A** TQ 240 411
Height gain	230 feet (70m)	**B** TQ 227 401
Approximate time	2 hours	**C** TQ 222 406
Parking	In front of St Nicholas Church	**D** TQ 223 417
Route terrain	Field edge and woodland paths	**E** TQ 234 419
Ordnance Survey maps	Landranger 187 (Dorking & Reigate), Explorer 146 (Dorking, Boxhill and Reigate)	

With more than 20 stiles this should win a trophy for having the most number of stiles on a short walk. The route, which starts from the village of Charlwood, passes through lovely sections of ancient woodland and despite its proximity to Gatwick airport this walk includes some tranquil and rural stretches.

Enter St Nicholas churchyard by the war memorial in The Street and pass to the left of the 11th-century church. Shortly after joining an enclosed path turn left to climb a stile **A** and follow the grassy path through a hedge gap. Bear right to climb another stile and keep along the left-hand edge of a paddock to climb another. Bear right, following waymarkers, through a hedge gap and hop over a stile in the field corner. Cross a track, climb another stile and keep ahead across a field to go over

Half Moon pub, Charlwood

a further two stiles in quick succession. Head straight across the next field and pass to the right of some farm buildings to reach a road. Here, turn left along a tarmac drive and almost immediately climb a stile on the right and follow the path, which runs parallel to the road, along the right-hand edge of a field. Negotiate another stile and cross the driveway to Russ Hill Farm before looking back for a distant glimpse of the runway at Gatwick airport.

Go along the road for 40 yds before rejoining the path alongside the hedge. At the signposts, climb a stile on the right and continue along the road for 200 yds, looking out for where you climb a stile on the right by a public footpath signpost **B**.

Pass to the left of a farm building and farmhouse, climb another stile and head to the far left corner of the field, hop over a stile and enter a delightful stretch of woodland, managed by the Woodland Trust. This is one of the

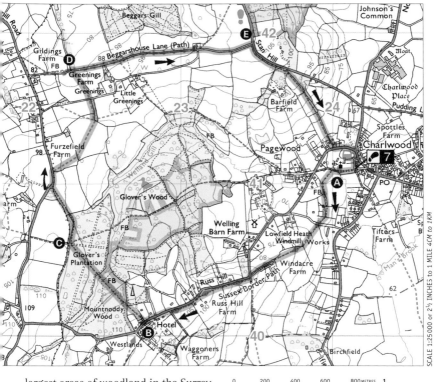

largest areas of woodland in the Surrey Weald and contains some unusual ferns with bluebells in springtime. Over to the right, is Glover's Wood, which is home to some rare species of tree in the Weald such as small-leaved lime.

The path descends by way of steps, crosses a wooden footbridge and ascends at the other side.

Follow the yellow waymarkers and on reaching a T-junction with a bridleway, at the edge of woodland, turn right **C** and keep ahead at a fork along a wide bridleway along the inside edge of the trees. The path soon becomes enclosed and comes out at a road. Turn right here and after 100 yds turn right at a public footpath signpost. Go over a stile and continue along the right-hand field edge, bearing left to a hedge gap to go over a stile and plank footbridge.

Bear diagonally left towards a house with white chimneys and a belt of trees. Ignore the first stile and keep to the left of a hedge to climb two stiles ahead, separated by a plank footbridge. Keep ahead across a field to climb another stile. Cross a farm track, hop over another stile, and keep ahead along the right edge of the next field, bearing right before it curves left, along an enclosed path. Go over another stile and plank footbridge and turn right **D** onto a byway that narrows and passes Greenings Farm, to join a lane.

Keep ahead and just before reaching a road (Stan Hill), turn right along a footpath running adjacent to the road **E**.

After crossing the driveway to Barfield Farm the path veers away from the road. Climb a stile and follow the enclosed path beside a wire fence then hop over the last stile of the walk and at the road, turn left, taking the first road on the right to return to the church. ●

Albury Park

Start	Silent Pool near Albury	**GPS waypoints**	
Distance	4½ miles (7.2km)	◢ TQ 059 484	
Height gain	425 feet (130m)	Ⓐ TQ 048 478	
		Ⓑ TQ 054 473	
Approximate time	2 hours	Ⓒ TQ 065 470	
Parking	Silent Pool car park, off the A25 near Albury	Ⓓ TQ 062 478	
Route terrain	Country lanes, parkland paths and bridleways		
Dog friendly	Keep on a lead through Albury Park where sheep graze		
Ordnance Survey maps	Landranger 187 (Dorking & Reigate), Explorer 145 (Guildford and Farnham)		

Although not lengthy this walk packs a punch with some delightful scenery starting with the village of Albury from where there are fine views of the church on St Martha's Hill. It continues through the rolling hills of Albury Park and passes by its wonderful little church before returning to Silent Pool.

For a glimpse of Silent Pool enter the woodland by the information board and pass Sherbourne Pond beyond which you'll find the pool. The water feeding the lake comes from springs in the Downs' lower chalk and since it has been filtered through the chalk it is utterly clear with a bluey, green hue. It is both serene and eerie. Legend tells the story of King John who took a shine to a young maiden who was bathing here. Unfortunately however, the feeling was not mutual and in the struggle that followed, she drowned.

Silent Pool was also linked to Agatha Christie in 1926 when it is thought she staged her own disappearance by leaving her car with the ignition on by the pond after an argument with her unfaithful husband. She was later found to be in Harrogate.

◢ Return to the car park, cross the A25 and continue along the roadside

path of the A248 and follow it over the River Tilling Bourne. The path curves right into Albury village passing the fishing lakes, Weston House and a large house with tall and ornate chimneys, and then **The Drummond Arms** pub before reaching the post office and village stores. Albury was mentioned in the *Domesday Book* when it already had a mill and a church.

Turn left along Church Lane Ⓐ. Follow the road as it curves left past the bowls club, to a memorial cross to the Duchess of Northumberland. Opposite this is the Church of St Peter and St Paul, built in 1842 when the villagers were forced to move from their homes to an adjacent hamlet after the owners of Albury mansion decided to develop a park around it and close the village church. When the new owner, banker Henry Drummond arrived he had a new church built for the villagers. His daughter married the Duke of Northumberland, and the family still has links with Albury.

Where the lane ends continue along an enclosed bridleway, bear right at a fork and at a hedge gap there is a wonderful view across to St Martha's Church on the hilltop. Keep ahead to a T-junction and turn left **B**.

Bear right at a clearing to follow the bridleway across two tracks to come out onto a lane. Pass to the right of the triangular green, cross the road and continue along Park Road opposite, which runs along the edge of Albury Heath. After passing a row of houses on your right, cross the road and follow the public footpath to the left of the kissing-gate **C**.

Go through a metal gate and enter the 150-acre Albury Park, which was once the original medieval village of Albury. Follow the well-waymarked path through the park, signposted 'Old Church', to arrive at a kissing-gate **D**. Go through and head across the grass to the church. This lovely Saxon church was closed in 1841 when the villagers had to move and was left to decay until 1921 when it was rescued. Nowadays the Churches Conservation Trust cares for it and a 15th century wall painting of St Christopher and its simple, uncluttered interior make this a very special place. Outside, the setting is equally lovely with ancient trees surrounding the church, which looks down over the banks of the River Tilling Bourne below.

From the church continue along the metalled drive running parallel with the Tilling Bourne over to your right. At the road turn right, in the direction of Dorking, then bear right to retrace your steps to the car park at Silent Pool. ●

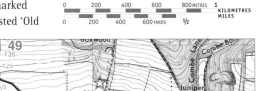

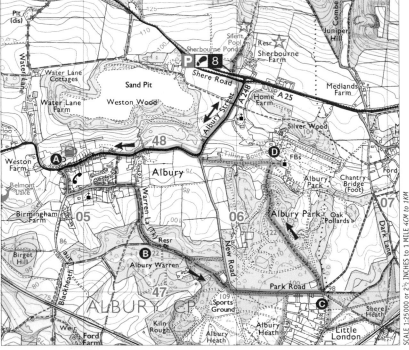

Cranleigh

		GPS waypoints
Start	At the sports pavilion, Cranleigh	<ul><li>TQ 059 388</li><li>Ⓐ TQ 056 387</li></ul>
Distance	5 miles (8km)	Ⓑ TQ 047 383
Height gain	150 feet (45m)	Ⓒ TQ 039 377
Approximate time	2 hours	Ⓓ TQ 045 369
Parking	Car park at the sports pavilion, off Knowle Lane	Ⓔ TQ 056 372
Route terrain	Meadow paths, rutted lanes and stretches along two minor roads	
Ordnance Survey maps	Landranger 187 (Dorking & Reigate), Explorer 134 (Crawley and Horsham)	

This is an easy stroll with a level course which passes through beautiful meadows, along the trackbed of the former Horsham to Guildford railway and a little-used path flanked with wild flowers by the Wey and Arun Junction Canal (like the railway, also disused) to follow a cross-country track known as Lion's Lane.

From the car park at the sports pavilion, off Knowle Lane follow the concrete drive back to the entrance at Knowle Lane, turn left and after 100 yds pass beside a gate on the right Ⓐ onto a field path along the left side of a beautiful meadow containing some ancient oak trees. When this path reaches Alfold Road turn left and follow

Old railway line

it for ¼ mile before turning right Ⓑ onto the drive to Utworth Manor.

Follow this bridleway towards the attractive old house as far as the pond. The bridleway bears left here to cut off the corner of a field: head for a large ash tree on the right-hand side of the field to join a track following the edge. Continue along the hedgeline and cross a footbridge with a blue waymarker, on the right. Bear left diagonally across a meadow and keep ahead, below the bank of the canal on your right. This is the Wey and Arun Canal, which opened in 1816 and was used to transport timber before the canal closed in 1870 after the arrival of the railway in 1865. There is dense woodland to the left and a companion waterway may

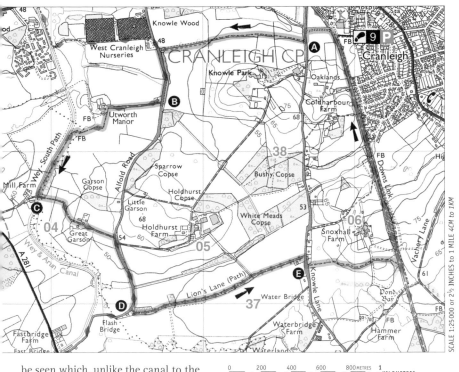

SCALE 1:25000 or 2½ INCHES to 1 MILE 4CM to 1KM

be seen which, unlike the canal to the right, is well filled with water. Continue along the canalside path, peppered with wild flowers, and at Mill Farm turn left and cross an old bridge, **C**.

The path follows the right-hand edge of two meadows to reach another old manor house, Great Garson, which is timbered and very attractive.

Go straight on through a wooden gate onto the drive to the house and follow this past a pond to reach a road. Turn right and when the road bends right take the byway to the left **D**, just before Fastbridge Cottage, which winds through a small patch of woodland. This is Lion's Lane, a delightful but deeply rutted old road, which provides nearly a mile of pleasant, sheltered walking. Where this ends at a road turn right and pass Snoxhall Cottage before turning left **E** and crossing a redundant stile onto a field-edge path and follow waymarkers eastwards to the dismantled railway. Climb a set of steps

at the embankment and turn left to begin the final leg of the walk back to Cranleigh. You are now walking on the Downs Link, a 36-mile footpath that links the North and the South Downs. The section you are on is part of the line, which once ran between Horsham and Guildford. In 1922 there were seven trains in each direction on week days, and the journey from Cranleigh to London Bridge took just over two hours. As the path nears Cranleigh look out for a concrete signal post surmounted with the remains of a semaphore signal in the 'clear' position. Cranleigh was the bed of an inland fresh water lake during prehistoric times and soon you will pass a cricket ground beneath which excavations have uncovered a bed of fossilised winkle shells commonly called Sussex Marble. The car park is ahead of you. ●

Churt Valley

Churt Valley

		GPS waypoints
Start	Churt	🔲 SU 854 385
Distance	5 miles (8km)	Ⓐ SU 857 388
Height gain	525 feet (160m)	Ⓑ SU 864 390
Approximate time	2½ hours	Ⓒ SU 867 378
Parking	Parking area in front of St John The Evangelist Church	Ⓓ SU 867 372
		Ⓔ SU 862 365
Route terrain	Undulating woodland paths, quiet lanes, two steep climbs	Ⓕ SU 854 379
Ordnance Survey maps	Landranger 186 (Aldershot & Guildford), Explorer 133 (Haslemere and Petersfield)	

The Churt Valley is an ancient area in the south west of Surrey and the name Churt first appeared in a document dated 688 when the King of Wessex gave some of his land to the religious authorities. This walk follows some quiet lanes and footpaths with a couple of steep climbs along the edge of woodland, later skirting Beacon Hill and following a stream to pass Barford Mill before returning by the village green.

🔲 Facing the church from the parking area, turn right and at the lane turn left and follow this to a public footpath sign opposite Old Kiln Cottage. Turn right and go through a kissing-gate Ⓐ and follow the enclosed path beside a fence, to go through a gate. Keep ahead through two more gates and bear left along the driveway to Old Kiln Farm.

This is one of the farms in Churt that lies on a fertile strip of soil called Bargate Sandstone – outside this area only gorse, bracken and heather can survive in the poor heathland soil.

At the end turn right along Jumps Road and then right again into Crabtree Lane Ⓑ. At the T-junction turn left and then right along Old Barn Lane.

Not far from here is the location of Bron-Y-De, where David Lloyd George lived for more than 20 years when he retired. He was Prime Minister during the First World War and introduced the pension system for those of 70 years of age and above for which they received five shillings per week (25p today). Despite the poor soil, he was a determined gardener and irrigated the land, planted fruit trees, grew vegetables and sold the produce from a farm shop.

At the end of Old Barn Lane turn right along Green Lane and just before the road curves to the right, turn left at a public footpath sign Ⓒ and go through a kissing-gate onto a delightful uphill stretch along the edge of woodland. Keep ahead as another path joins yours from the left and bear right at a Y-junction, now with a young plantation on your right.

Where the path curves left look out for an easily missed path on the right by a waymarked post Ⓓ. Follow this footpath as it descends steps to the edge of a golf course. Cross the narrow fairway and keep ahead, steeply uphill the other side to reach a three-way path junction. Turn left, cross the track to the clubhouse and bear right at a waymarked post to arrive at Churt Road. Cross this and follow the enclosed footpath opposite down to a kissing-gate. Continue downhill, turning left at a track and just in front of another kissing-gate turn right along a grassy downhill path towards the left-hand field corner where there is a three-way footpath sign **E**.

Turn right along a path running parallel with the road and after going through a kissing-gate turn right along

the road. Where the road bends to the right bear left along a bridleway, past houses and onto an enclosed, leafy track that passes to the right of Barford Mill, one of three mills in the area and used for making corn – now a private house. In Churt, mills were an integral part of the community and Barford employed 100 people and was still in use in the early 20th century.

Bear left **F** along a lane – the building to your right here is Kitts Farm which dates from Saxon times and is built on the fertile strip of Bargate Sandstone – keep ahead and at the next

0	200	400	600	800 METRES	1
					KILOMETRES
					MILES
0	200	400	600 YARDS	½	

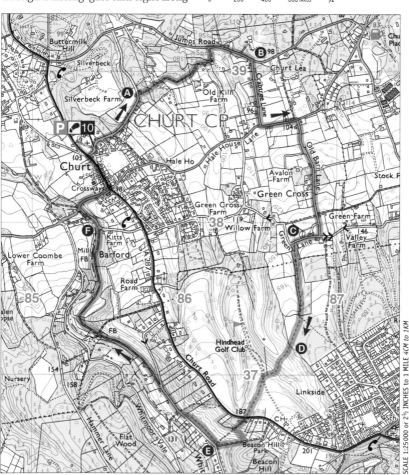

SCALE 1:25 000 or 2½ INCHES to 1 MILE 4CM to 1KM

main junction, cross Barford Lane and turn right to follow the roadside path. At the crossroads by **The Crossways**, an ancient pub, turn left and pass a row of shops to reach the war memorial on the village green. Cross the green to return to the parking area in front of the church. ●

Memorial near church in Churt

MEN OF CHURT WHO DIED
THAT HONOUR MIGHT LIVE
1914 - 1918

ARCHIE BOWERS. Pte. E. Surrey Regt.
FRANK BOWERS. Pte. The Queen's
H.J. CANE. Pte. Royal Fus.
JAMES CLARK. Pte. M.T. Corps
THOMAS CLARK. Sergt. Essex Yeo.
A.T.W. CONSTABLE. Major Essex Regt.
L.A. CRIDDLE. Pte. The Queen's
H.E. GOODYEAR. H.M.S. Black Prince
ERNEST HARRIS. Pte. R.A.S.C.
DUNCAN HOOK. 2nd Lieut. Lancs. Fus.
ROBIN HOOK. 2nd Lieut. Lancs. Fus.
VALENTINE HOOK. Capt. The Queen's
ALBERT E. HITCHINGS. Pte. Middx. Regt.
CEDRIC LARBY. Pte. London Regt.
HERBERT LARBY. Pte. Hants. Regt.
THOMAS LARBY. Pte. The Queen's
DESMOND TROUTON. Capt. R.F.A.
F.T. TROUTON. Capt. Scott. Rifles
ALBERT VOLLER. Gunner R.G.A.
J.W. WRIGHT. Pte. The Queen's

1939 - 1945

P.J.N. ADSHEAD. Pilot Officer R.A.F.V.R.
E.A. ALDERTON. Gunner R.A.
NICHOLAS A. ANSDELL. Flying Officer R.A.F.
WILLIAM T. BOYCE. P.O.W. Royal Navy
PATRICK W. BROWNE. Major The Kings Regt.
A.H.T. BRYANT. Sergt. A.P.T. Corps
R.E. HARDMAN-JONES. Act. Comdr. Royal Navy
JOHN H. HARRISON. Pilot Officer R.A.F.V.R.
R.A. HOFMAN. Capt. Norfolk Regt.
G.S. PETTIS. Flt. Engr. Sergt. R.A.F.
P.H. RICHMOND. Sergt. R.A.F.
W.A.B. TREVOR. D.S.O. Major R. Tank Regt.
ARTHUR HENLEY. Pte. R. Hants. Regt.
P.R.F. WALKER. Major R.A.

Chobham Common

Start	Staple Hill, Chobham Common	GPS waypoints	
Distance	5¼ miles (8.4km)	🖉	SU 972 647
Height gain	165 feet (50m)	Ⓐ	SU 979 650
Approximate time	2½ hours	Ⓑ	SU 989 645
		Ⓒ	SU 991 637
Parking	Staple Hill car park	Ⓓ	SU 993 631
Route terrain	Woodland paths, bridleways	Ⓔ	SU 972 632
Ordnance Survey maps	Landranger 175 (Reading & Windsor), Explorer 160 (Windsor, Weybridge & Bracknell)		

A foray through Chobham Common, one of the best remaining examples of lowland heath; rich in wildlife and invertebrates, and home to one of Britain's rarest creatures, the red-barbed ant. The route also offers a chance to spot kingfishers and passes an ancient monument, The Bee Garden Earthwork, at Albury Bottom.

🖉 From the Staple Hill car park, cross the road, pass between two waymarked posts and a few steps farther turn left along a sandy bridleway. At a Y-junction with a path leading from Longcross car park turn right Ⓐ and bear left at the next two forks. The bridleway gently ascends through an area of gorse, conifers and birch and you can hear the distant hum of traffic on the busy M3. Chobham Common is one of the best sites in the country for spiders, ladybirds and butterflies and on warm, summer evenings you may even hear a nightjar.

Keep ahead at a path crossing and just after passing a yellow waymarker on the left, is a T-junction. Turn left here, along the bridleway Ⓑ past a wooden fence to reach another path junction. Bear right and keep ahead along the main path as it meanders to the right through conifers to skirt a more open section of the common before re-entering woodland. At a fork

keep left and pass to the left of a wooden fence to reach a lane. Turn left along the lane for about 100 yds and then turn right at a bridleway signpost Ⓒ.

At a waymarked post at a fork beside a metal gate take the right-hand footpath and follow this as it passes first a field and then goes over a board walk. At a fork bear right to pass through a wooden barrier by a yellow waymarker, and at the next fork turn right Ⓓ and climb a stile.

Continue along the left-hand field edge path, climb a stile and keep ahead across the field to climb another stile. Continue along the right-hand edge of a field, hop over another stile and then the path becomes enclosed between paddocks, passing to the right of Blackberry House. Turn right just past this at a public footpath sign, climb a stile and bear left across the field to cross a wooden footbridge over a stream – look out for kingfishers along

Chobham path

this stretch - then turn right along a grassy path beside a wooden fence. Go over a stile and follow this delightful, enclosed path.

Go through two kissing-gates and the path joins a tarmac drive to arrive at a road. Turn right here, bear left at the triangular green to cross Red Lion Road and turn right at a 'Footpath No 15' signpost to continue through woodland rich in fungi, bearing left at a fork.

At a path crossing keep ahead and at the fork bear right and soon you will pass the backs of houses. Bear right at the next fork to reach a T-junction then turn right along the bridleway **E**. Pass to the right of a long strip of paddocks and farmland, keep ahead at a path crossing and at the main path junction turn right. After a few paces turn left towards a fingerpost, then bear left and keep ahead – do not turn right at the next black waymarker – and head towards a copse, later skirting the right side of it.

Head across grassland steadily uphill, passing the Earthwork of The Bee Garden, which was probably built by prehistoric farmers. Walk through the

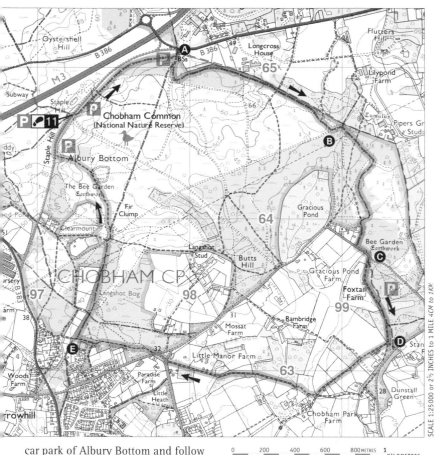

car park of Albury Bottom and follow the narrow path on the opposite side, which runs parallel to a road on your left. Pass a wooden barrier next to the road, and at a set of waymarked fingerposts, turn left and cross the road to return to the car park. ●

Chobham Common

The Devil's Punchbowl

		GPS waypoints
Start	Hindhead	✍ SU 890 357
Distance	5¼ miles (8.4km)	Ⓐ SU 887 364
Height gain	605 feet (185m)	Ⓑ SU 887 369
Approximate time	2½ hours	Ⓒ SU 889 386
Parking	National Trust car park on the eastern edge of Hindhead, off the A3	Ⓓ SU 894 386
		Ⓔ SU 896 384
		Ⓕ SU 896 368
Route terrain	Gravel paths, sandy tracks, some steep descents and climbs	Ⓖ SU 900 359
Ordnance Survey maps	Landranger 186 (Aldershot & Guildford), Explorer 133 (Haslemere & Petersfield)	

The Devils' Punchbowl is probably Surrey's most celebrated natural feature and this large heather-filled basin was formed naturally by many springs. This route follows its western rim before dropping down to cross to its eastern side. A footpath leads to Gibbet Hill – a superb viewpoint and the site of a grim hanging. From here it is a straightforward route back to Hindhead. There are some steep and lengthy climbs on this walk.

Punch Bowl viewpoint

Facing the **National Trust café** behind the car park bear right, past an information board and the roughly surfaced track leads to a viewpoint with waymarks on top. Bear left and you will pass to the right of a fence and a well-placed seat with views over the natural amphitheatre. At a path junction turn right **A**, and pass a green metal barrier and a cattle-grid and head for Highcomb Copse on a broad track along the western edge of the Punchbowl.

Here there is open woodland with a frequent thick carpet of bracken.

Occasional views show the ground falling away dramatically to your right. At a waymarked tree stump post where the track forks three ways, take the right-hand fork **B**, on a path which is a detour to an excellent viewpoint from where you can see Highcomb Bottom and the Hog's Back. A memorial to the brothers of W.A. Robertson stands here. Both were killed in the First World War, and the Devil's Punchbowl was given to

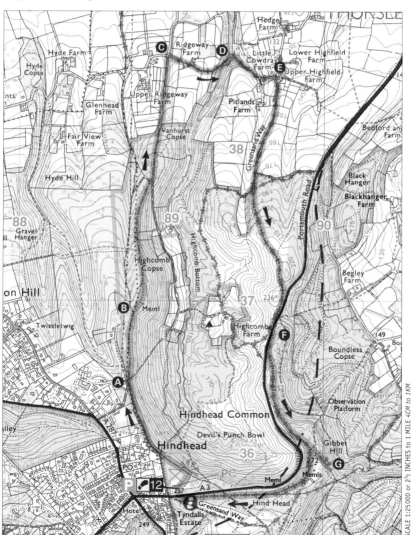

the National Trust by their family to commemorate the men's sacrifice.

Continue past the monument to return to the main path, which descends gently. At another waymarked tree stump at a crossing of paths keep straight on and bear right at a fork. The path begins to descend more steeply through Vanhurst Copse and in doing so becomes narrow and enclosed. Go through a gate and a National Trust boundary marker shows where you leave Trust land.

The steep path can be heavy going after wet weather, but eventually it reaches Hyde Lane. Turn right here ❻ to pass Ridgeway Farm. Now there is another steep section down a path with high banks to a footbridge over a small stream ❶.

Do not go over the stile ahead but bear right up a track, forking left to reach a lane. Turn left again and then right ❸ after 100 yds, waymarked Greensand Way. A long climb up a shady track with a good surface brings you to a National Trust signboard where the track divides. Bear right here, continuing to follow the Greensand Way, and then left a little farther on. Go straight over the footpath junction, which follows almost immediately. The climb continues, but at last the scenery changes to heathland and the sandy path reaches the top of the ridge, where there are views, which overlook the Punchbowl.

Before reaching the road, there is a diversionary path to the right, which avoids the churned bridleway and allows better views of the Punchbowl. Follow the path down, pass beside a cattle-grid and cross the road with care. Take the path opposite signposted 'Quiet Lane' ❺ by a Hindhead Common sign and continue uphill past a green metal barrier and a milestone. At a pair of green bollards with yellow rings turn left to the triangulation pillar of Gibbet Hill ❼.

Milestone

Back in 1786 an unknown sailor was murdered nearby and the culprits were executed and their bodies left to the mercy of the elements on the hilltop gibbet, a kind of cage with chains. A granite Celtic cross was erected nearby to ward off any evil spirits.

Retrace your steps and continue uphill and you will soon pass to the right of the Sailor's Grave. Keep ahead and cross the road back to the National Trust car park. ●

Tilford and Waverley

		GPS waypoints	
Start	The village green in Tilford	🖋	SU 873 434
Distance	5¾ miles (9.2km)	Ⓐ	SU 874 434
Height gain	575 feet (175m)	Ⓑ	SU 872 449
Approximate time	3 hours	Ⓒ	SU 870 455
Parking	Parking area beside the village green in Tilford	Ⓓ	SU 875 453
		Ⓔ	SU 878 459
Route terrain	Open heathland and heather, woodland tracks and a steep climb	Ⓕ	SU 885 458
		Ⓖ	SU 893 443
Ordnance Survey maps	Landranger 186 (Aldershot & Guildford), Explorer 145 (Guildford and Farnham)		

You will follow in the footsteps of medieval monks on this walk which passes three pubs, the medieval bridge at Tilford, the ruins of Waverley Abbey and the colourful heathland of Crooksbury Common. It also ascends to Crooksbury Hill where there is a steep climb. Tilford's quaint village green is home to a museum of rural life, the Barley Mow pub, and a timbered institute designed by Edwin Lutyens.

🖋 From the parking area beside the village green, bear right to cross the medieval bridge, once used by the monks from nearby Waverley Abbey. Turn left at the bridleway sign Ⓐ and follow this as it climbs steadily.

Bear left to join a tarmac road, pass Tilhill House, and then continue along an enclosed path to a fork by a waymarked post. Take the right-hand path, which passes a couple of farmhouses to arrive at a road. Cross this and continue along the path opposite, through conifers and turn left at the T-junction Ⓑ to reach a road.

The ruins of Waverley Abbey, the oldest Cistercian abbey in the country is off to the left, just past a sharp left curve in the road Ⓒ. The monks started Surrey's wool industry and converted the surrounding forests into grazing land and arable fields. You can see the remains of the 13th century vaulted refectory and some walls once belonging to the

Crooksbury Common

Chapter House and some of the stonework was used in the building of Loseley House *(see Walk 14 Compton and Loseley Park)*. The abbey's demise was already underway before Henry VIII got his hands on it but this once flourishing riverside ruin is now the perfect spot for a picnic.

Retrace your steps to where you emerged onto the road and keep ahead and just after the entrance to Keepers Cottage Stud turn left at a public bridleway sign **D** and follow this to another road.

Turn left along the road for 200 yds and then turn right, to cross Crooksbury Hill car park and follow a steep path on the left that eventually reaches the

triangulation pillar (trig point) at the top of Crooksbury Hill **E**.

The views from the top of the hill on a clear day are stunning and from here you can see over southwest Surrey and across to the South Downs.

Stand with your back to the memorial plaque on the triangulation point and follow the path ahead, downhill, bearing right at an obvious fork along a narrower path and soon you will come to a path crossing. Turn right along the bridleway, marked by a blue-painted post, to a road. Cross the road and join a track opposite at a bridleway sign that passes houses, to reach a T-junction **F**.

Turn right here and follow the long, sandy path across Crooksbury Common with its magnificent conifers and heather. Look out too for the red and

Medieval bridge in Tilford

white spotted fly agaric fungi in autumn near birch trees. This site is an important area for the smooth snake and sand lizards, which have been introduced here and are both protected species.

Keep ahead at a crossways and continue, past houses, to Farnham Road. Cross this with care and turn right at a public byway sign **G**, passing to the right of **The Donkey** pub. At a cross track bear left, past Ravenswing, and keep ahead until you reach a road beside a house called Whitmead. Turn

right and follow the lane downhill – you can see the River Wey through trees to your left – and the path later ascends to a triangular green. Bear left here along a lane and at the next road turn left again towards Tilford's bridge and return to the car park. You might look out for an 800-year-old oak tree beside the village green said by William Cobbett, the political journalist, MP and reformer, to be the finest tree he ever saw. ●

Compton and Loseley Park

Start	Watts Cemetery, Compton	**GPS waypoints**	
Distance	6 miles (9.6km)	✒ SU 956 474	
Height gain	445 feet (135m)	Ⓐ SU 967 478	
		Ⓑ SU 991 483	
Approximate time	3 hours	Ⓒ SU 985 476	
Parking	Small parking area in front of Watts Cemetery, in Down Lane, Compton. Alternative parking is at Watts Gallery	Ⓓ SU 966 475	
		Ⓔ SU 959 468	
		Ⓕ SU 954 473	
Route terrain	Sandy bridleways, woodland paths		
Ordnance Survey maps	Landranger 186 (Aldershot & Guildford), Explorer 145 (Guildford and Farnham)		

This reasonably level walk traces the North Downs Way eastwards before passing through the grounds of historic Loseley House and later Compton village with its interesting buildings and 10th-century church. Watts Chapel is a unique memorial to the Arts and Crafts Movement and well worth a visit.

✒ With your back to Watts Cemetery and Chapel turn right along Down Lane and just before the car park to Watts Gallery and **tearoom** turn right along a bridleway to follow the North Downs Way.

The gallery, which re-opens in spring 2011 after refurbishment, displays over 500 works of the painter and sculptor, G F Watts, including the original plaster cast of *Physical Energy,* which sits in Kensington Gardens.

Keep ahead as the path narrows and passes between trees to a crossing of paths Ⓐ. Keep ahead along a charming woodland stretch initially beside the Loseley Estate nature reserve, all the way to a Y-junction. Bear left and then right, leaving the bridleway and continuing uphill following the North Downs Way fingerposts. Climb a stile beside a gate and the path curves left and then right along a tarmac road. The

road later becomes a rough track and then a grassy path beside a field and eventually runs along the backs of houses on the outskirts of Guildford. Cross the road and turn right Ⓑ, along

St Nicholas Church, Compton

a path that climbs above the road and becomes enclosed.

Cross a road and join another enclosed path ahead at a public footpath sign. The buildings to your left are Mount Browne, the headquarters of Surrey police and former home of the Marquess and Marchioness of Sligo.

At a path T-junction turn right **C**,

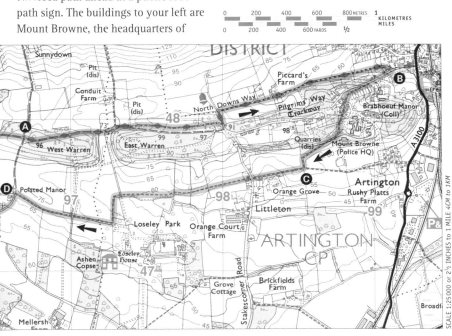

Window in Watts Chapel

Loseley House is open from May until August and there are good views of it to be had as you keep the lake on your left and go through a kissing-gate to walk along the left edge of a field. Climb a stile in the field corner, cross a track and keep along the enclosed path as it curves first left and then right to join a stoney track.

Where the track ends in front of a farmhouse, Little Polsted, turn left **D** along a lane. Keep ahead at a small triangular green, and just before reaching the T-junction with the B3000, turn right at a public footpath sign across Compton village green **E**. The name Compton means 'valley farm' and it was first recorded in the *Domesday Book*.

Cross the road (Spiceall) and continue through Compton, passing the village hall, **The Harrow pub** and an attractive timbered cottage called White Hart, which dates from the 15th century and was once an ale house.

Soon after this is the ancient 10th-century Church of St Nicholas and its fascinating history including a graffiti self portrait of a Norman knight who it's thought went to the Crusades and returned around AD1140. The old 'scratch sundial' outside would have indicated to the villagers when services were taking place and the font is made from 'carstone' a type of rock found south of the Hogs Back.

Continue along The Street and turn right into Down Lane **F**, just before the main T-junction to return to Watts Cemetery where George Watts is buried. A visit to the extraordinary Victorian chapel built by his wife, Mary, and the villagers is a wonderful way to end the walk. The interior of the terracotta chapel is simply stunning with swirling rich reds, blues and golds in a symbolic fusion of Celtic, Art Nouveau and Romanesque styles. ●

along an enclosed field edge path that later joins a tarmac drive to pass a row of cottages. Cross over a road and continue ahead through a kissing-gate and straight across the next two fields. Go through another kissing-gate to enter a lovely picnic area with tables beside a lake in front of Loseley House. The More family has owned this estate, built in 1560 with stone from Waverley Abbey after the dissolution, since the 16th century. Sir William More was an advisor of Queen Elizabeth I and John Donne, who after marrying a young Ann More without her father's permission paid the price by spending a year in prison. Inside, the Great Hall contains panelling from Henry VIII's lavishly designed Nonsuch Palace and carvings by Grinlin Gibbons and bedrooms include the ones used by Elizabeth I and James I during their visits.

Farley Heath

		GPS waypoints
Start	Farley Heath	🔲 TQ 052 448
Distance	6 miles (9.6km)	Ⓐ TQ 055 436
Height gain	575 feet (175m)	Ⓑ TQ 048 435
Approximate time	3 hours	Ⓒ TQ 063 426
Parking	Farley Heath car park, off Farley Heath Road	Ⓓ TQ 056 454
Route terrain	Forest tracks, rutted lanes	
Ordnance Survey maps	Landranger 187 (Dorking & Reigate), Explorer 145 (Guildford and Farnham)	

This peaceful walk follows bridleways and tracks through Farley Heath and a number of copses, including a Christmas tree plantation and passes the site of a Roman Temple. There are some steady climbs, a series of steep steps and a stretch along a deeply rutted lane.

🔲 Begin by facing the road and bear right across the car park joining a bridleway then cross the road and follow the sandy bridleway ahead. Cross a track and at a fork bear right. As the main sandy track swings sharply left, continue ahead on a downhill path that eventually reaches a T-junction Ⓐ.

Turn right along this rutted lane (Madgehole Lane) until it meets a tarmac road beside houses. Turn left Ⓑ in the direction of Winterfold through this peaceful valley, past Madgehole Farm. At Madgehole continue through its garden and turn right along an enclosed uphill path which soon runs alongside a plantation of Christmas trees. Cross a track and keep ahead following bridleway signs, to join the Greensand Way. This is a most pleasant and peaceful section of the walk. Cross the road and go up a set of steep steps opposite and continue as the path weaves through the woodland. Bear right at a fork and keep ahead as the path first descends and then climbs to reach a car park (No. 5). Here, turn left Ⓒ.

To the right is Winterfold Hill, part of the same range of hills as Leith Hill, which belongs to the Lower Greensand spanning out into the Surrey Weald. The dramatic Winterfold greensand hills is a secluded, undulating area founded on greensand with a densely wooded landscape containing large areas of Spruce and Scot's Pine.

Cross the road and join the path opposite. Bear right and then turn left in front of the wire fence and the path then runs to the left of the garden to Winterfold Cottage.

You are now crossing the old Roman Road that led north west from Stane Street. You will cross the line of the road again on Ride Lane, just after the junction with Madgehole Lane a little farther along the walk.

Now bear left and at a rough track, turn left. Cross Row Lane and continue along the bridleway, turning right to join Ride Lane – after 100 yds you will cross the Roman Road again – and follow this sometimes deeply rutted lane all the way to Farley Green. Eventually, you will pass Farley Hall and its timbered farmhouse. Bear left at the village green and follow Farley Heath Road **D** and after ½ mile bear right back to the car park.

As you enter the car park you'll find the site of the Roman Temple on the right. Thought to date from AD 100 and

Farley Heath

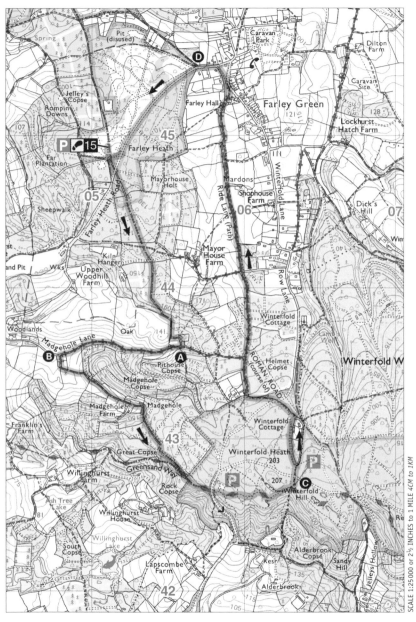

used as a market the temple's elevated position was chosen carefully to ensure it could be seen across the heathland. It was still visible in the 16th century and excavations in 1939 uncovered 1,000 small coins, possibly wishing well offerings. Martin Tupper who lived in nearby Albury excavated the site and some of the artefacts are now on display in the British Museum. Today, some of the Roman stonework traces the exact ground plan of those original ancient buildings.

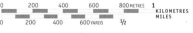

Bramley and Farley Hill

		GPS waypoints
Start	Bramley	✔ TQ 009 447
Distance	6½ miles (10.4km)	Ⓐ TQ 010 450
Height gain	490 feet (150m)	Ⓑ TQ 006 457
Approximate time	3 hours	Ⓒ SU 993 453
Parking	In front of the Catholic church in the High Street, next to Bramley library	Ⓓ SU 986 446
		Ⓔ SU 997 447
		Ⓕ SU 996 442
		Ⓖ TQ 010 431
Route terrain	Bridleways, woodland paths, country lanes	
Ordnance Survey maps	Landranger 186 (Aldershot & Guildford), Explorer 145 (Guildford and Farnham)	

This attractive route from Bramley includes part of the Downs Link and then climbs steadily with some far reaching views from Farley Hill. Although prone to mud after heavy rain it's shady and so an ideal walk for warm, dry days. There are some tranquil stretches and quiet bridleway paths.

Along the edge of East Waters woodland

📷 With your back to the church turn right along Bramley's high street and after a few paces, turn right. Turn left to cross a stream and pass a plaque in a small park dedicated to the Robertson family who introduced electricity to the village in the 1920s. Pass the village hall and at the road, turn right. Just after the old level crossing gates turn left at a public footpath sign in the direction of Guildford and Godalming Ⓐ.

You are now on the Downs Link, a 32-mile (54km) long bridleway, cycle route and footpath that links the North and South Downs Way using a railway line that closed in 1966. It's very atmospheric and a white platform shelter with display boards tells how enemy aircraft hit a train packed with Christmas shoppers during the Second World War. The railway itself opened in 1865 and came under the axe a century later when Lord Beeching recommended that more than 4,000 route miles were given the chop to make the organization more cost effective. The railway's loss is certainly our gain.

The path soon runs beside the River Wey and at the brick Tannery Lane bridge turn right and at the road, turn left to cross the bridge **B**.

After 50 yds bear right along the gravel track beside houses to the road (A281). Cross this and at the public footpath sign opposite the gates to Gosden House School, join a path through Gosden Common. Cross a

driveway and then a lane and follow the footpath passing to the right of Gosden Farm House. Keep ahead and pass beside a barrier to a road. Bear right and at the T-junction turn left, and then bear left before the bridge into Unstead Lane. A few paces farther, turn right over a stile beside a public footpath sign, **C**.

Keep ahead, beside a wire fence, go over a stile, shortly followed by another one. Turn right to join an attractive

Beside the Millpond

bridleway and continue, past a farm to a path T-junction **D**.

Turn left to a path junction at a public footpath sign and turn left along the bridleway, which runs uphill along the edge of woodland. After 500 yds turn left at a post waymarked 'The Fox Way' and continue to ascend Farley Hill. The path curves right with views to the left of a training ground for horses and farther afield, the county town of Guildford. Keep ahead as the path descends to join a track and then a road where you turn right **E**.

Continue uphill along Foxburrow Hill Road, looking out for where you turn left at a house called Wood End **F**.

Bear left at a public footpath sign in front of gates and follow this as it descends via a track to a lane. Turn left along the lane and turn right at a bridleway sign to walk along the left edge of a millpond. Bear right past Eastwater House along an uphill stretch on the edge of woodland that opens onto a landscape of undulating hills. Continue along another uphill stretch to a public bridleway sign beside a house, and turn left, **G**.

The bridleway initially borders the edge of woodland before crossing fields and descending through Hurst Hill to a road. Take the road opposite (Ricardo Court) and keep ahead joining a public footpath and, where this meets a road, bearing left to return to the start. ●

Leith Hill and Friday Street

Leith Hill and Friday Street

		GPS waypoints	
Start	Below Leith Hill, near Coldharbour village	🔲	TQ 147 432
Distance	6½ miles (10.5km)	**Ⓐ**	TQ 142 432
Height gain	900 feet (275m)	**Ⓑ**	TQ 139 431
		Ⓒ	TQ 130 436
Approximate time	3 hours	**Ⓓ**	TQ 132 443
Parking	National Trust's Landslip car park	**Ⓔ**	TQ 126 442
		Ⓕ	TQ 128 458
Route terrain	Woodland paths and tracks, some steep ascents	**Ⓖ**	TQ 135 456
		Ⓗ	TQ 139 441
Dog friendly	Keep under control where cattle graze through Dukes Warren	**Ⓙ**	TQ 147 437
Ordnance Survey maps	Landranger 187 (Dorking & Reigate), Explorer 146 (Dorking, Box Hill & Reigate)		

At 965 feet (294m) Leith Hill is not only the highest point in Surrey but also the highest in south east England. It is a magnificent viewpoint, one of a series that crowns the well-wooded greensand ridge a few miles south of the North Downs. This walk is mostly through the lovely pine and beech woods and over areas of sandy heathland that is characteristic of greensand country, and although fairly hilly in places it is relatively undemanding. However, do follow the route instructions carefully; the large number of tracks and paths in this area, much of which is owned by the National Trust, can be confusing at times.

🔲 Begin by taking a path that leads up from the car park, following the first of a series of signs with a tower symbol on them, towards Leith Hill Tower. At a track turn right Ⓐ to head quite steeply uphill. Bear left in front of a gate marked 'Bridleway' at a junction and climb again to reach Leith Hill Tower Ⓑ. This was built in 1766 by Richard Hull of nearby Leith Hill Place to compensate for the hill just failing to top the 1,000ft mark; the extra height pushes it to 1,029ft. There is a small admission charge to the tower, from where there is one of the finest and most extensive panoramas in the south east: northwards across to the North Downs and beyond that to London and the Chilterns, and southwards over the Weald to the South Downs and the English Channel.

Just past the tower the path forks. Take the right-hand path here, at a second fork take the left-hand one and at a third fork take the left-hand one again. Shortly after, a well-defined path joins from the left. Continue ahead for about ½ mile, following the straight main path across Wotton Common to reach a crosstrack Ⓒ. Turn right here along a fairly straight path and after ½ mile bear left at a T-junction to a lane Ⓓ. Turn left and almost immediately turn right, at a public footpath sign, along a path that keeps along the inside edge of woodland, with a fence on the right.

On the edge of the woodland go through a kissing-gate and follow a path across a field to go through another kissing-gate at the far end. Continue along an enclosed path to the right of houses, soon re-entering woodland, and descend, by an old wire fence on the left, to a crossroads **E**. Turn right along a track that winds through the beautiful woodlands of Abinger Bottom, briefly emerging from the trees to reach a lane. Keep ahead along the lane and opposite the drive to a house called St Johns bear right to continue along a wooded track. After passing a barrier the track becomes a tarmac lane, which you follow through the charming and secluded hamlet of Friday Street to a T-junction passing the **Stephan Langton** pub.

Turn right to pass across the end of the millpond, a former hammer pond and one of many in the area that were created to power the hammers of the local ironworks up to the time of the Industrial Revolution. The view across it nowadays could hardly be more tranquil. On the far side, turn half right **F**, at a public footpath sign, along a path that heads uphill away from the pond, passing to the left of a National Trust sign for Severells Copse, and continue steadily uphill to a lane. Cross over, keeping ahead to cross another lane and continue along the path in front. Take the right-hand path at a fork – not easy to spot – and head downhill along a sunken path, bearing slightly right on meeting another path to continue downhill, curving left to a lane.

Turn left through Broadmoor, another attractive and secluded hamlet, and opposite a riding centre turn sharp right **G**, at Greensand Way and public bridleway waymarks, onto a track. Keep on this straight and broad track through Broadmoor Bottom for one mile and, 700 yds after passing to the right of

Friday Street, a lovely hamlet in Surrey

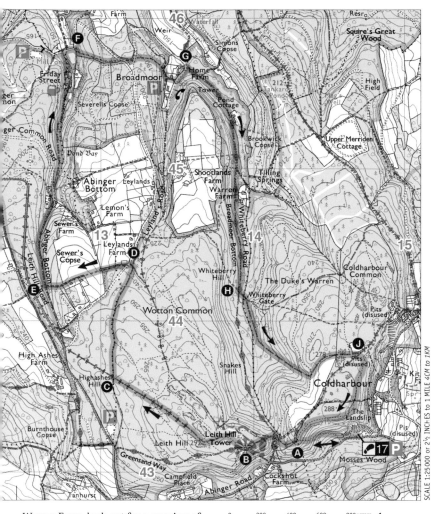

Warren Farm, look out for a crossing of paths and tracks by a bench **H**. Turn half left here onto a path; after a few yards cross a stream, by a National Trust sign for Duke's Warren, and a few yards farther on at a fork take the right-hand path. This is a most delightful part of the walk, initially between woodland on the right and more open sloping heathland dotted with trees on the left. Later the path re-enters woodland and heads steadily uphill, finally curving left to a junction.

Bear left for a few yards to a fork and take the right-hand track, following the direction of a blue waymark and pass through a gate to leave Dukes Warren, to

emerge alongside the right-hand edge of the cricket pitch on Coldharbour Common. Just after the cricket pavilion turn half right at a National Trust information board along a path with a green wooden post signposted 'Coldharbour Walk', **J**. Ignore all side turns and follow the green waymarkers all the while. To the left there are grand views over the Weald to the South Downs on the horizon. Opposite a barrier on the right **A**, turn left to rejoin the outward route and head downhill back to Landslip car park. ●

Ripley Green and the River Wey

			GPS waypoints
Start	At the cricket pavilion, Ripley Green		🗒 TQ 053 569
Distance	7 miles (11.2km)		Ⓐ TQ 055 570
Height gain	Negligible		Ⓑ TQ 056 578
Approximate time	3 hours		Ⓒ TQ 054 585
Parking	Ripley Green car park just off the High Street		Ⓓ TQ 053 592
			Ⓔ TQ 045 588
			Ⓕ TQ 043 584
Route terrain	Riverside paths, towpaths, woodland bridleway		Ⓖ TQ 050 578
			Ⓗ TQ 039 574
Ordnance Survey maps	Landranger 187 (Dorking & Reigate), Explorer 145 (Guildford and Farnham)		Ⓙ TQ 034 568
			Ⓚ TQ 039 569

This is a good level walk starting from Ripley Green and heading north to pass Ockham Mill and Pyrford Lock. The return portion follows the River Wey with views over towards the remains of an Augustinian priory.

🗒 With your back to the cricket pavilion turn right and keep ahead beside houses to a tarmac drive. Turn left here and pass between wooden posts to a waymarked post Ⓐ and continue along the bridleway along the edge of Ripley Green. Maintain direction following blue bridleway signs – the trees also have blue rings painted on them – and go over a wooden footbridge to cross the first section of water. Cross another footbridge and at Mill Lane turn left Ⓑ, and follow the lane past the former Ockham Mill and turn right at the public footpath sign beside the mill building. The Earl of Lovelace, who was a Victorian entrepreneur, built this in 1862 – look out for his coronet, which can be seen at either side of the overhanging timbered section.

Go over a stile and follow the enclosed tree-lined path to cross a long, wooden footbridge over the River Wey. Running parallel on the right is the white bridge of Wisley Golf Course.

At the T-junction turn right Ⓒ, now with the river to your left, and continue along the towpath to Pyrford Lock Ⓓ.

The River Wey navigation is almost 20 miles long and runs from Guildford to the Thames at Weybridge. It was the first artificial waterway in Britain and Pyrford, which means a ford by a pear tree, is one of its 12 locks.

You'll pass lots of narrowboats along this stretch and will eventually arrive at the lock and the popular pub, **The Anchor** that is adjacent. Cross the bridge before the pub and continue along Lock Lane past Pyrford Marina and at the T-junction turn left and after 100 yds turn right at a public footpath sign. After passing Pyrford Green House the grassy path runs along the edge of farmland to a three-way signpost **E**.

Turn left here and keep ahead at the next two public footpath signposts and, with a row of pylons to the right, continue to the next path junction **F**. Here you can keep ahead visiting the tiny village and its church.

Pyrford's small Norman church was built around AD1150 and here you can see some original wall paintings of scenes from Christ's Passion and of pilgrims preparing to sail to Spain. Since William the Conqueror granted the manor of Pyrford to Westminster Abbey it is believed that the Abbot of Westminster built the church.

Retrace your steps to **F**, turn right over a stile beside a metal gate along a grassy path between fields and go over a stile onto a lane. Turn right along Warren Lane for about 300 yds and turn left at a public footpath sign beside a metal gate, along an enclosed tarmac drive that runs to the right of a golf course. The path continues to a tributary of the River Wey by Walsham Lock. Turn left to cross the footbridge over the river and then turn right and

keep ahead with the river on your right to cross the bridge over Walsham Weir .

At the end turn right to follow the towpath and just after the next footbridge, look over the meadow on your right for a view of the remains of Newark Priory, an Augustinian house founded at the end of the 12th century by Ruald de Clane and his wife Beatrice of Send. When Henry VIII dissolved the monasteries the surrounding land became part of his hunting ground. It is now privately owned.

The path crosses Newark Lock – the remains of the priory can be seen clearly through the trees here – and continues to a road. Look out for little owls, which inhabit the trees in this area and turn left to cross the bridge then turn right to rejoin the riverside path **H**.

Just in front of Papercourt Lock turn left **J**, along a grassy path following a line of oak trees and cross a footbridge. Surrey Wildlife Trust manages the Papercourt site, much of which is designated an SSSI. The lush area is a mixture of wet meadow, marsh and grazing. Bear half left and head across the meadow to reach an enclosed path to the right of a mobile bungalow, **K** and at the end of this path climb a stile on to a lane (Papercourt Lane). Turn left here, past **The Seven Stars** pub and at the B367 turn right and follow this all the way to Ripley Green where, just after the manor house of Dunsborough Park, you bear left along a path at the edge of the common and return to the car park. ●

The weir at Walsham

Limpsfield

		GPS waypoints	
Start	Ridlands Lane, near Limpsfield Chart	🖊	TQ 418 522
Distance	7 miles (11.2km)	Ⓐ	TQ 420 521
Height gain	590 feet (180m)	Ⓑ	TQ 436 522
Approximate time	3½ hours	Ⓒ	TQ 435 513
Parking	National Trust Ridlands Grove car park off Ridlands Lane	Ⓓ	TQ 429 513
		Ⓔ	TQ 429 508
		Ⓕ	TQ 422 507
Route terrain	Undulating woodland paths	Ⓖ	TQ 416 516
Ordnance Survey maps	Landranger 188 (Maidstone & Royal Tunbridge Wells), Explorer 147 (Sevenoaks & Tonbridge)	Ⓗ	TQ 406 518
		Ⓙ	TQ 416 521

An attractive route following part of the Greensand Way to the Kent border and later joining a section of the Vanguard Way. The directions must be followed closely between Ⓒ and Ⓓ. There are a few descents and a couple of steep climbs through areas of woodland.

🖊 With your back to the information board in the car park turn left down the lane and turn right at a public bridleway sign Ⓐ. Go through a gap in the trees on the right to pass in front of a barn and join a driveway. At the road turn left and keep ahead as the footpath becomes enclosed and veer away from the road. You are now on the Greensand Way. Cross a lane, turn left at the **Carpenters Arms** pub and cross another lane, all the while following Greensand Way waymarkers, bearing left at a waymarked post. Soon you will enter Titsey Foundation woodland where there is a good mix of silver birch and pine. Keep ahead until you reach a five-way path junction – just ahead, a few paces farther, is a stone marking the spot where the Greensand Way is equidistant between Hamstreet in Kent and Haslemere in Surrey – turn sharp right at the junction Ⓑ and keep along

the straight, woodland path, passing beside a gate to a road. Cross the road and continue along the public footpath opposite, which initially runs beside a metal fence, and then descends through the trees.

Keep ahead downhill as the path narrows to arrive at a tarmac driveway. Turn right along this Ⓒ and at a fork bear left along the waymarked Tandridge Border Path, bearing left again at the next fork to continue downhill.

Near here is a woodland house called The Cearne where D.H. Lawrence would visit when he was in the area. The house became a meeting place for writers and artists as well as Russian refugees.

At a track bear right past another waymarked post and Scearn Bank Farm, and where the road ascends through trees bear left along a narrow path, which shortly descends to a lane on the edge of Scearn Bank woodland .

Turn left here and keep ahead passing beside a wooden gate and later, to the right of a stone wall by houses and where the lane sweeps to the left just after Trevereux Stables, climbing a stile on the right **E**.

Walk along the right-hand edge of a field and at the top, as it curves left, look out for where you climb a stile on the right. Continue along the left edge of the field and in the corner hop over another stile and immediately turn right along the enclosed path. Climb another stile on to a lane, opposite which is a pond. Turn right, past Moat Farm and its nearby cottages, and just before Chartlands climb a stile on the right **F** and walk along the left edge of a field. Climb a stile in the corner and go over a plank footbridge then bear right across grass to join a gravel track to the left of a house.

Keep ahead, and although the footpath passes through a garden there is an alternative path to the left that skirts it. Cross a footbridge at the end of this enclosed path and turn left to climb over a stile. Keep along the left-hand edge of the field, hop over a stile in the top left corner to enter woodland and follow the path, past the backs of houses, to a gravel track.

Turn left **G**, and rejoin the Greensand Way and a few paces farther, at a path junction, turn right along the tarmac road opposite Arden Lodge and continue all the way to a road.

Cross the road and join the footpath opposite, which passes a house and descends along the edge of woodland, and climb a stile on to a road. Turn right here **H** and just before the road curves right, turn left at a public footpath sign into woodland, along a steep, uphill path. At the driveway to a school turn right and then right again at

the main road. At the T-junction turn left and then right into New Road and after a few paces join a path that veers right to cross Limpsfield Common.

The common lies on the Kent border on the Greensand Ridge and is dominated by woodland that is carpeted with bluebells in springtime. In the past few centuries grazing helped to keep the common as open heathland but a decline in this has encouraged scrub to appear and just a few patches of heath remain. The National Trust is now working to preserve these open areas and encourage wildlife to thrive here.

Keep ahead as the Greensand Way joins your path from the left and follow it uphill. At a tarmac track bear left to

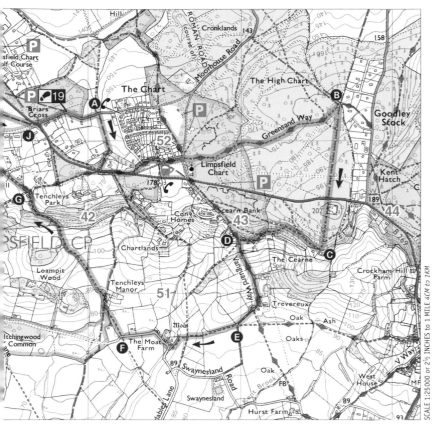

cross a road and continue along the path at a bridleway sign to pass the edge of a golf course and come out at Chapel Road **J**. Turn left, cross the main road (the B269) and turn left into Ridlands Lane to return to the car park. ●

Woodland near to Scearn Bank

Shabden and Upper Gatton Park

		GPS waypoints	
Start	Elmore Pond, Chipstead		
Distance	7 miles (11.2km)	✐ TQ 278 568	
Height gain	770 feet (235m)	Ⓐ TQ 276 561	
		Ⓑ TQ 285 558	
Approximate time	3½ hours	Ⓒ TQ 281 549	
		Ⓓ TQ 285 540	
Parking	Recreation ground	Ⓔ TQ 259 544	
Route terrain	Grassy field edge and cross-field paths	Ⓕ TQ 266 555	
		Ⓖ TQ 266 558	
Dog friendly	On a lead through grazing areas		
Ordnance Survey maps	Landranger 187 (Dorking & Reigate), Explorer 146 (Dorking, Box Hill and Reigate)		

This is a fairly long but well waymarked and easy to follow route with sweeping views of rolling fields and parkland. The walk has uphill stretches, passes The Long Plantation, and has numerous stiles.

✐ Leave the car park passing to the right of Elmore Pond and continue along the road for about ½ mile looking out for a public footpath sign on the left. Turn left Ⓐ and follow the path through trees to a road. Turn left and just past the gate to Noke Farm Cottage turn right at a public footpath signpost. Now go through a kissing-gate and follow the orange Shabden and Upper Gatton waymarkers along a tarmac drive and where this swings left, keep ahead across grass to pass a wooden barrier. Continue along the right-hand edge of a field and along a gently descending grassy path, and cross a track. Bear right through a hedge gap and then bear half left across the field to a stile at the top. Hop over this and a few paces farther, cross a track and go through a hedge gap then across a field to another waymarked post. Turn right here in front of it, still following the

orange waymarkers Ⓑ and follow the permissible path along the left-hand field edge. Go through two hedge gaps and at another orange waymarker, turn left initially along an enclosed path and then along the right-hand edge of a field alongside a copse. The path later becomes enclosed again before reaching a crossing of paths Ⓒ. Turn left, hop over a stile and keep ahead across a field to climb another stile.

Bear right and then left through trees and keep beside a hedge on the left to climb another stile on to a lane. Turn right along the lane and look out for where you turn left to go through a kissing-gate at a public footpath sign. The path passes Rose Cottage and Boors Green Farm to go through another kissing-gate on the left. Keep along the right-hand edge of the field and go through another kissing-gate and then turn left along a farm track. Turn right at a public footpath sign to go through a kissing-gate and keep to the left of a hedge to go through another kissing-gate before the path enters a young plantation. Go through a kissing-gate and ahead, on the other side of the M25, is the south section of Gatton Park.

From this spot at the top of Ashtead Hill you have a fine view of the North Downs ridge.

Here, a permissive path allows you to turn right along the field edge but the right of way continues downhill so head left to the edge of Marling Glen Wood towards the traffic on the M25 and at a public footpath sign **D** just before a wire fence, turn right and walk uphill now heading for the left edge of woodland and go through a gap in the trees. Turn left in front of a metal gate and follow the enclosed path between a hedge and a wire fence, all the way to a road.

Cross the road and keep ahead through the grounds of quirky **Fanny's Farm Shop** – this also has a **café** - to a bridleway sign beside an orange waymarker and turn right.

Head across the field towards Upper Gatton Wood and just before you reach a public footpath and bridleway signpost, turn left to skirt the top edge of this field. Climb a stile in the corner and follow the path through a lovely stretch of woodland, bearing left at a waymarked post to continue along a wide grassy path. Hop over a stile beside a brick air raid shelter and continue along the right edge of a field.

Over to the left is the white Upper Gatton Park House. Climb a stile in the field corner and keep along a short enclosed path beside a road to a house. Cross the road and at the public footpath signpost opposite, hop over a stile and bear slightly left to follow the path across a field. Keep to the left of a row of trees by a wire fence to climb another stile, on to a road.

Cross this, go through the gate opposite and keep along an enclosed path, which later runs alongside a wire fence between fields. Keep ahead at a three-way signpost and descend to a path junction beside a stile **E**.

Turn right, now leaving the Shabden and Upper Gatton circular walk, and continue along the field edge path, go through a kissing-gate in the corner and head across a field to go through two more kissing-gates, separated by a lane. Cross a field making for the top left corner, go through another kissing-gate and join an enclosed path on the left edge of woodland. At a metal gate turn right, hop over a stile and follow another enclosed path beside paddocks, turning right to a lane just after a house. Turn left along the lane and at the T-junction turn right along White Hill. A few paces past Pigeonhouse Farm turn left through a hedge gap by a public footpath sign **F**, and climb a stile. Keep ahead and where the wire fence ends continue to head uphill across a field. Climb the stile and continue through the woodland. At a wide crossing turn left uphill and at a fork bear right to a set of waymarkers. Turn right here **G**, through woodland and keep ahead following the orange waymarkers through The Long Plantation. This area was planted in the 1700s and is a Site of Special Scientific Interest in recognition of its grassland and chalky woodland. In the past intensive farming has taken its toll on this area but recent practices have returned it to its former wildlife-friendly splendour.

The path continues uphill, past grazing sheep, and where it runs adjacent to a road, turn left at an orange waymarker, now along the top section of the field with fabulous views of The Long Plantation and continue to a gate. Go through and bear right along the farm track, uphill through trees, passing to the right of Shabden Park Farm, to reach a road. Turn left and retrace your footsteps to the start of the walk. ●

Albury Downs and St Martha's Hill

		GPS waypoints
Start	Newlands Corner	◢ TQ 043 492
Distance	7 miles (11.2km). Shorter version 2¼ miles (3.6km)	Ⓐ TQ 033 489
		Ⓑ TQ 033 486
Height gain	985 feet (300m). Shorter version 375 feet (115m)	Ⓒ TQ 021 486
		Ⓓ TQ 003 483
Approximate time	3½ hours (1½ hours for shorter version)	Ⓔ TQ 003 480
		Ⓕ TQ 021 478
Parking	Car park at Newlands Corner off A25	Ⓖ TQ 027 477
		Ⓗ TQ 028 483
Route terrain	Some steep climbs, farm tracks and enclosed paths	Ⓙ TQ 035 485
Ordnance Survey maps	Landranger 186 (Aldershot & Guildford), Explorer 145 (Guildford & Farnham)	

*From the starting point on the Albury Downs near Guildford –
part of the North Downs and one of its finest viewpoints – this
walk twice descends below the crest of the downs and twice
climbs to regain it. Open downland interspersed with frequent,
attractive wooded stretches makes for a good, varied walk,
especially when allied with superb and extensive views from the
highest points at Newlands Corner and St Martha's Church.
Of the two climbs the first one that ascends St Martha's Hill is
quite steep and strenuous; the second that returns you to the
start is more gradual. The shorter version includes only the latter,
easier ascent.*

◢ Starting with your back to the
refreshment kiosk, turn half-right, head
downhill across the grass to pick up a
stoney path and bear right along it, soon
passing a yellow waymarker post,
indicating that this is part of the North
Downs Way. Now follow a splendidly
scenic path, below the edge of woodland
on the right and with extensive views over
the downs to the left. At a fork take the
left-hand path and do the same at the
next fork, keeping along the right-hand
edge of woodland. Soon the path enters

the trees, bends to the left and heads down
to a lane Ⓐ.

Cross over, go up some steps and turn
left, at a North Downs Way sign, along an
enclosed, wooded path that heads downhill, parallel to the lane on the left, to a
T-junction of paths in front of a house Ⓑ.

*At this point those who wish to do the
shorter version of the walk should turn left
to rejoin the main route after 200 yds at
Ⓙ below.*

Turn right here, leaving the North
Downs Way, along a path that keeps by

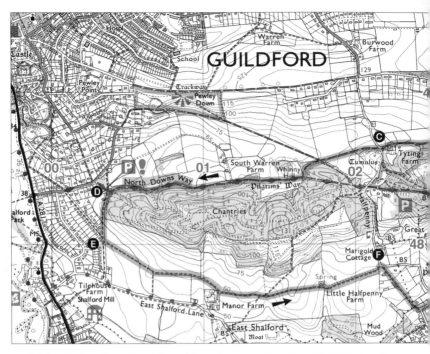

the left-hand edge of woodland; later this path broadens into a track. Continue, passing through a farmyard to reach a lane **C**. Cross over, take the enclosed track ahead at a public bridleway sign, and at a crossing of tracks by a Pewley Down information board, keep ahead into woodland. The track curves left to a T-junction where you turn right, rejoining the North Downs Way along a track between wire fences. Over to the right,

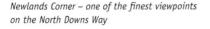

Newlands Corner – one of the finest viewpoints on the North Downs Way

houses on the edge of Guildford can be seen. The track keeps along the right-hand edge of Chantry Wood – along this section the North Downs Way coincides with the Pilgrims' Way – finally going to the right of a cottage to a crossing of tracks **D**. Turn left along an enclosed path beside Chantry Lodge, still keeping along the right-hand edge of Chantry Wood, and on reaching a road bear left.

After 50 yds turn left **E** over a stile at a public footpath sign and walk across the middle of a field, later continuing by a hedge on the right. Turn right through a hedge gap near a farm, turn left to continue in the same direction, now along an undulating track, eventually going through a gate onto a lane **F**. Turn right and almost immediately right again, at a public footpath sign, to continue along an enclosed path which descends to a lane. Turn left here and where the lane

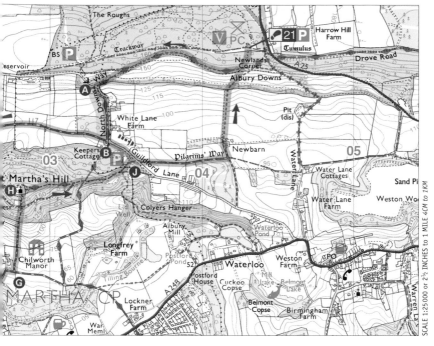

bends sharply to the left keep ahead,
passing to the left of a lodge. Continue
along a gravel track through the grounds
of Chilworth Manor.

The track curves left, keeping to the
right of the manor house. At a fork turn
right and go along a rough track between
fences. After 50 yds turn left **G**, at a
public footpath sign, along an enclosed
path which heads steeply up St Martha's
Hill, the most strenuous part of the walk
but leading to one of the finest views in
Surrey. On the upper slopes of the hill the
path crosses a sandy track and continues
up to St Martha's Church **H**, 573ft high
and a superb viewpoint looking out over
the North Downs, Guildford, along the
greensand ridge and across the Weald to
the distant South Downs. This isolated
hilltop church (the parish church of
Chilworth) was rebuilt in 1850, partly from
the stones of the original Norman church
that stood on the site. It is one of the major
landmarks on the North Downs Way.

At the church, turn right along a broad,
sandy track that heads downhill, with

0	200	400	600	800 METRES	1	
					KILOMETRES	MILES
0	200	400	600 YARDS	½		

grand views along the greensand ridge
ahead, continuing through woodland to
reach a junction. Keep straight ahead,
passing to the right of a ruined wartime
pillbox, and at a junction of three tracks
take the left-hand one that leads through
a car park to a lane **J**.

Here you rejoin the shorter route. Turn
right and after 50 yds bear left along a
straight, fence-lined path which runs
below the crest of the Albury Downs on
the left, later continuing along the left-
hand edge of woodland. Once more this is
part of the supposed line of the Pilgrims'
Way. At a public bridleway sign turn left,
along another enclosed bridleway. Pass to
the left of a farmhouse and at a yellow
waymarked post beside the barn head up
across the field towards Albury Downs.
At the top go through a gate and continue
uphill, bearing right across grass to rejoin
the stoney path, which will take you back
to Newlands Corner. ●

Witley to Haslemere via Chiddingfold

Witley to Haslemere via Chiddingfold

		GPS waypoints
Start	Witley Station	☑ SU 948 379
Distance	7¼ miles (11.6km)	Ⓐ SU 950 373
Height gain	490 feet (150m)	Ⓑ SU 954 369
Approximate time	3½ hours (plus return trip on train)	Ⓒ SU 958 358 Ⓓ SU 942 344
Parking	Witley Station car park off Combe Lane	Ⓔ SU 936 344 Ⓕ SU 926 336
Route terrain	Grassy paths, valleys and some country lanes	Ⓖ SU 906 326
Dog friendly	Some stiles not suitable for large dogs	
Ordnance Survey maps	Landranger 186 (Aldershot & Guildford), Explorer 133 (Haslemere & Petersfield)	

A linear route following a beautiful valley of rolling hills and streams, passing the pretty village of Chiddingfold and belts of woodland before joining the Serpent Trail in Haslemere and ending with a 10-minute rail journey back to Witley. Trains run hourly (South West Trains tel. 08457 484950).

☑ From Witley Station car park walk down Station Approach and at the crossroads turn right. After 600 yds turn left at a public footpath sign Ⓐ and climb a stile, then cross a paddock to climb another one. Keep ahead through a belt of trees to climb a stile and head half left, across a field, to a stile by a hedge gap. Hop over the stile and go across the plank footbridge into the next field, heading for the left of farm buildings opposite, and climb another stile.

Bear left past Noddings Farm and at the public footpath signpost turn right to climb a stile Ⓑ. Keep initially along the right-hand edge of the field, and then head downhill towards a metal gate. This is a beautiful stretch of the walk with rolling hills and green pastures.

Go through the gate, cross a narrow field and hop over the stile and cross an earth bridge to enter woodland of Hartsgrove Hanger. Cross another earth bridge and head gently uphill, go through a kissing-gate, then stay along the right-hand edge of a field towards the backs of houses. In the field corner go through a kissing-gate and then along an enclosed path to a road. Turn left and follow the road as it curves right and keep ahead at a junction. Turn right into Coxcombe Lane Ⓒ and at the end is Chiddingfold's pretty village green with its pond, church and **The Crown** pub. For 300 years the village was famed for its glassmaking and most of the properties around its green date from the 14th to 16th centuries. Turn right passing to the left of St Mary's

Village pond, Chiddingfold

Church, and then turn right along Mill Lane.

Ignore the public footpath signs to the right and keep ahead past Upper Sydenhurst along the tarmac bridleway, which skirts the edge of woodland. The path bears left in front of a gate to Hollyhurst and runs beside a wire fence. Keep ahead all the way to a lane and turn left **D**.

Just before the road curves left over a bridge, keep ahead at a bridleway sign and after passing farm buildings turn left over a stile **E**.

Bear half-right across the field, hop over a stile along the wooden fence, and cross the next field, then keep along the left-hand edge. Ignore the stile on the left and climb the stile in the field corner beside a yellow waymarked post.

A few paces farther, keep ahead at another yellow waymarker and continue along the edge of Frillinghurst Wood. Cross a wooden footbridge and head uphill and at a fork by a public footpath sign bear left through a copse, following the yellow waymarked posts, to continue along the left edge of a field. At the path junction, go through a hedge gap on the left and bear right to another set of signposts in front of a fishing lake **F**.

Turn left and follow the path as it curves right to skirt the edge of the lake and passes to the right of farm buildings. Cross a lane and go through the kissing-gate opposite beside Holdfast Cottage. Keep along the right edge of a field, go through a kissing-gate and turn right past houses, along an enclosed path. Go

Wooded valley near Hartsgrove Hanger

ahead joining the Serpent Trail, which was opened in 2005. Cross a wooden footbridge, go through the gate and head straight across a field. Go through a hedge gap and keep ahead through a gate. Bear right to join a gravel track and follow this all the way to Haslemere's main road **G**.

The town grew when it became more accessible after the London to Portsmouth railway opened in 1859. Many well-known artists and writers liked to visit including George Eliot, Alfred Lord Tennyson, Conan Doyle and George Bernard Shaw.

Look out for a plaque on the town hall dedicated to General James Oglethorpe, a local MP from 1722 to 1754, who founded the colony of Georgia in the United States of America.

Turn right here and keep ahead, following signs to the station in Haslemere where you should catch the train one stop back to Witley. ●

through another kissing-gate into Swan Barn Farm, an area rich in wild flowers and managed by the National Trust. The path then follows the right-hand edge of a series of fields linked by kissing-gates, plank footbridges and steps, to enter Witley Copse and Mariners Rewe at a National Trust sign. The path continues to the right of a wire fence and bears left at a fork to reach a three-way footpath sign next to a National Trust one on the edge of the copse. Keep

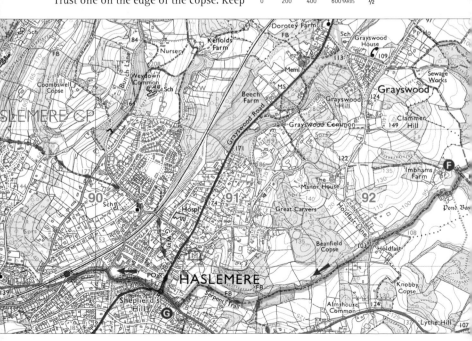

Outwood and its Mill

Start	Outwood	
Distance	7½ miles (12km)	
Height gain	345 feet (105m)	
Approximate time	3½ hours	
Parking	National Trust car park opposite the windmill	
Route terrain	Grassy field edge paths, plenty of stiles	
Dog friendly	On a lead from **C** as livestock are in fields	
Ordnance Survey maps	Landranger 187 (Dorking & Reigate), Explorer 146 (Dorking, Box Hill and Reigate)	

GPS waypoints

- ✍ TQ 326 456
- Ⓐ TQ 327 456
- Ⓑ TQ 319 472
- Ⓒ TQ 317 494
- Ⓓ TQ 335 491
- Ⓔ TQ 333 473
- Ⓕ TQ 339 456

This walk starts from the site of Britain's oldest working windmill and there are plenty of stiles and kissing-gates to negotiate. The picturesque route features rolling farmland and passes along the edge of Outwood Common and then crosses the railway line before returning by cross-field paths and along edges of woodland.

✍ From the car park head back towards the road but just before reaching it head diagonally left across the common and at a tarmac road turn left **Ⓐ**, and pass a garage and then a house called Treetops where the road ends. Keep ahead to climb a stile and join a grassy path, then go through a hedge gap and along the right-hand edge of the next field. Go over another stile in the field corner and head across the next field and go through a kissing-gate. Maintain direction, crossing another field and hopping over the stile then keep along the left-hand field edge and through a kissing-gate on to a farm track. Turn immediately right **Ⓑ** and not far along turn left at a public bridleway sign, and pass to the right of Burstow Park Farm.

At the next path junction, keep ahead, go through a kissing-gate and across another field where you negotiate another kissing-gate and a stile, and bear left, passing through a hedge gap to follow the right edge of the next field. Go over another stile, shortly followed by a kissing-gate and a footbridge. Cross another field with a kissing-gate and cross a wooden footbridge with a stile and bear half left to a hedge gap. Turn right here, initially beside a hedge before veering left towards a stile in the middle of the wooden fence at the top of the field.

Cross another field and go over a plank footbridge and a stile to join an enclosed path between the backs of houses, and hop over another stile. Turn left and at a path junction at a track to a farm, keep ahead along the public footpath going over a series of stiles before ascending a set of steps at the railway embankment. Cross the railway

track with care and go over another stile and then along the left-hand edge of the next two fields, separated by stiles. The M23 is now above you and hidden by the trees. Just before the third stile, by a concrete track on your left,

turn right along the left-hand edge of a field, **C**.

Climb a stile then keep along the left-

Village of Outwood

hand edge of a field, climb another stile and follow the grassy path as it swings to the right of a copse, and then bear half left across the field to go through a gate. Keep along the left edge of the field, hop over a stile, cross a road and go along the gravel drive to Laundry Farm. Follow an enclosed path beside a field, cross a brook and continue along the edge of woodland passing to the right of a field. The path curves right just after a metal gate **D**, and joins a concrete drive to pass Cuckseys Farm. Bear left at a yellow waymarker and head downhill along a lovely fern-lined path to the left of Poundhill Wood, later passing through an attractive area of woodland. The path becomes enclosed again until it reaches a field. Here, keep ahead and after 50 yds the path curves sharp left, past a pond to join a stoney track **E**.

Go through a hedge gap and follow the track as it bends to the right, along the left edge of a field, all the way to a concrete track. Turn left and immediately right along the gravel bridleway, which passes Lodge Farm, and joins a wide track. At a junction bear right and follow the right-hand field edge along the bridleway, which later curves right.

Go through a gate and at the path junction by a waymarked post turn right **F**.

When you reach the road turn right along Gayhouse Lane – it's from this lane that you'll get a good view of the windmill, built in 1665. After 500 yds just opposite a public footpath signpost, climb a stile on the right and head diagonally left across a field to the midway hedge gap. Go over a stile here and keep along the right-hand field edge.

This section belongs to Harewood Estates and was once part of a medieval 13th century deer park. Ahead is Outwood Windmill, the oldest working windmill in Britain and Grade I listed.

Go over a stile in the field corner and cross the car park of **The Bell** pub and at the road turn left. The windmill is over to the left if you would like to visit it but to return to the car park, turn right at the public footpath sign and cross the common. ●

Frensham Common

		GPS waypoints	
Start	Frensham Little Pond	✎	SU 856 418
Distance	7¾ miles (12.5km)	Ⓐ	SU 862 412
Height gain	360 feet (110m)	Ⓑ	SU 866 407
Approximate time	3½ hours	Ⓒ	SU 861 406
Parking	Frensham Common Little Pond car park, off Priory Lane	Ⓓ	SU 859 405
		Ⓔ	SU 853 399
		Ⓕ	SU 855 394
Route terrain	Woodland paths, quiet lanes, one short, steep climb	Ⓖ	SU 880 403
		Ⓗ	SU 886 413
Ordnance Survey maps	Landranger 186 (Aldershot & Guildford), Explorers 133 (Haslemere & Petersfield) and 145 (Guildford and Farnham)	Ⓙ	SU 881 418
		Ⓚ	SU 868 425

There are few walks, which better illustrate the varied nature of Surrey's landscape than this one. At the beginning and end there is pleasant walking in coppiced woodland, while the middle section goes through an area of forestry reminiscent of parts of Scotland. Much of the return leg, along the ridge of Kettlebury Hill, gives wide views northwards to Guildford and beyond.

✎ From the Frensham Common Little Pond car park off Priory Lane, turn right along the road and shortly

The Flashes

after passing Pond Cottage turn right at a public footpath sign to skirt the pond.

Frensham Little Pond, which used to be called Crowsfoot was built in 1246 on the orders of the medieval bishop

William de Raley and contained bream, pike and carp.

As the path winds its way through pine trees it's hard to imagine a more pleasant way to begin a walk. Where the path forks at a fence on the left bear left **A** and follow this out of National Trust land. The enclosed path becomes a track between fields, with a tree nursery to the right. Keep straight on over another track – there are initially pine woods to the left and a field to your right. Pass through a barrier and at a path junction turn sharp right **B** onto a bridleway. This soon meets a road – turn left onto this – and passes through swampland. Cross the ford, where there is a footbridge and immediately after this **C** leave the road by bearing left to follow the blue waymarked post of a bridleway. At a path junction after Gray Walls **D** turn left onto another bridleway and keep on this main track to pass to the rear of Lowicks House with its large pond. The bridleway gradually ascends to a main path junction. Turn left here **E** past a paddock on the left and the sandy track descends past the driveway to Crosswater House, after which it becomes surfaced.

Continue along this lane to pass nurseries and then turn left along a permissive track **F**. This leads into an area known as the Flashes, a heathery basin which would not look out of place in the Scottish highlands. This local nature reserve is dominated by purple moor-grass, cottongrass, ling and mosses and the bog here is an important area of peatland. The track enters wood again having skirted this area of emptiness, although since it has been replanted with conifers its character may soon be lost.

Keep along the bridleway to pass the Devil's Jumps, four Bronze Age tombs

dating from around 500BC which can be seen in the meadow to the right, just before the track meets a junction of tracks. They are conical greensand outcrops known as the High Jump, Middle Jump and Stony Jump, which contain ironstone and are an important habitat for reptiles. Again keep straight on, staying with the blue waymarked bridleway (no.P5)

Houses can now be seen on top of the hill ahead, and soon after the track

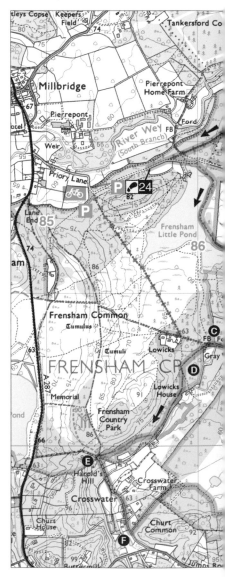

meets a road on the outskirts of Rushmoor.

Turn left along the main road and then after 100 yds turn right down a track leading to a military training area. Cross a stream, turn left onto the track beyond it and then right at the next junction of five tracks. Bear left when the track divides, and carry straight on over the next junction, climbing steeply to reach the bridleway on the crest of Kettlebury Hill **G**. Turn left onto this.

The walking is delightful on top of the sandy ridge, although noise from army firing ranges can sometimes be heard. Bear right at a bridleway fork to keep to the crest. Look out for the distinctive shape of Guildford Cathedral to the north at the next junction, which is known as the Lion's Mouth **H**.

There is a meeting of five ways here.

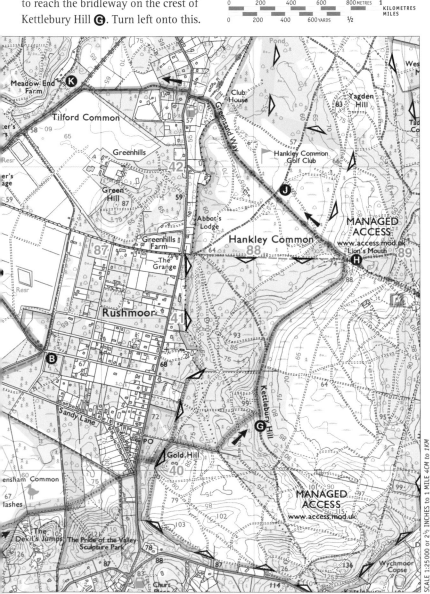

Turn left along the path to the left of wooden posts and descend to a bridleway sign where this time seven paths meet.

Turn half left onto bridleway 101 (as shown by a short post with an arrow) and go straight across Hankley Common golf course for 500 yds to another set of crosstracks . Keep ahead here along the Greensand Way, past a driving range and through trees to reach a wide track. Turn right and keep ahead past the club house to the road where you'll find the **Duke of Cambridge** pub. Turn right and almost immediately turn left at a bridleway sign along a gravel drive, passing paddocks to bear left along a byway **K**.

Keep ahead, passing to the right of Tilford Common and enjoy this lovely, undemanding end to a walk that has covered some of the best countryside in Surrey. The leafy track emerges on to a road where you turn right and the car park at Frensham Little Pond is on your left.

Frensham Little Pond

Gomshall and the Abingers

Start	Gomshall	**GPS waypoints**	
Distance	8 miles (13km)	✐ TQ 088 478	
Height gain	755 feet (230m)	Ⓐ TQ 092 476	
		Ⓑ TQ 112 482	
Approximate time	4 hours	Ⓒ TQ 121 483	
Parking	Gomshall Station car park	Ⓓ TQ 126 461	
		Ⓔ TQ 105 460	
Route terrain	Woodland paths and enclosed tracks, some quiet country lanes	Ⓕ TQ 091 470	
Ordnance Survey maps	Landranger 187 (Dorking & Reigate), Explorers 145 (Guildford and Farnham) and 146 (Dorking, Boxhill and Reigate)		

There are some excellent views – and plenty of stiles – along this walk which covers a mix of farms, woodland and heath beneath the North Downs escarpment. After a gradual ascent to Abinger Roughs the route crosses the Tilling Bourne and then climbs once more. There are some splendid views across the valley and a couple of great pubs in equally scenic settings.

✐ Turn left out of the station car park into Station Road and pass under the railway bridge and after 500 yds turn left along an enclosed track (Beggars Lane) at a public byway signpost Ⓐ.

After 200 yds look out for a narrow, uphill path through trees on the right and follow this, through a gate and along an enclosed path with some good views on the left over the valley towards Netley Heath. Cross a lane and pick up the path opposite to go through a gate and then keep ahead on a gradual ascent, following blue waymarkers to enter the woodland of Broomy Downs.

At a junction of paths keep ahead along the main bridleway, through an area called Abinger Roughs, following an undulating route through the trees to pass a memorial to Samuel Wilberforce. This marks the spot where the son of the abolitionist was killed after falling from

his horse in 1873. At a road cross over and follow the bridleway (not the footpath to the right of it), Ⓑ along an enclosed path with fields to the left.

At the junction of paths just past Park Farm bear right uphill along a footpath that goes across grass towards woodland Ⓒ. Go through a kissing-gate into Deerleap Wood and follow the enclosed path past a church, all the way to the A25 at Wotton. The Saxon church stands alone overlooking the North Downs and has some unusual carved heads around the porch door including those of King John and Archbishop Stephan Langton. Inside is the tomb of John Evelyn, the diarist.

Cross the road and head through the car park beside **The Wotton Hatch** pub then climb a stile and make for the top right corner of the field to climb another stile. Follow the sunken path downhill to cross the Tilling Bourne stream and ascend the other side. Go over another stile and follow the path as it heads uphill through Damphurst Wood, ignoring side paths. At a T-junction before a series of weirs, turn left and continue along a wide path and hop over a stile to reach a path crossing **D**.

Turn right and cross an old stone bridge over the Tilling Bourne and bear left along an uphill track, to a road. Turn right along the road and look out for where you join a path on the right, beside a sunken bridleway. At a road turn right, and then first left along a tarmac lane. At the T-junction turn right to pass **The Abinger Hatch** pub, which is in a peaceful spot, opposite the church and the tiny village green. Turn left by a public footpath sign in front of the church, go through the lychgate and pass to the left of the church to go through a gate and along an enclosed

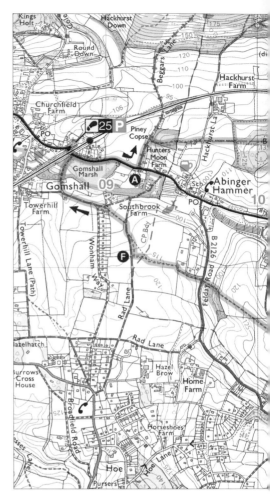

Woodland at Gomshall

path that skirts Abinger Manor and its motte. Go through a kissing-gate and keep ahead, initially along the left edge of a field, after which the path becomes a track and curves left before Raikes Farm. At a fork bear left and continue beside a wire fence along a narrow path. Go down steps and at a lane, turn left.

At the end of this lane is **The Volunteer**, another charming pub with an attractive garden, but to continue the walk, turn

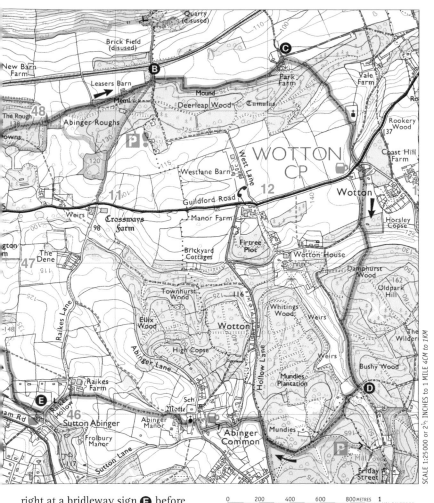

SCALE 1:25000 or 2½ INCHES to 1 MILE 4CM to 1KM

right at a bridleway sign **E** before
reaching the pub. Follow this as it
swings right at a set of iron gates, and
continues along the right-hand edge of
a field. Cross a track and bear left along
the bridleway and at the next three-way
signpost, turn left to join a public
footpath. Keep beside the wire fence on
the left, climb a stile and maintain
direction as the path descends across
farmland. Climb another stile and
continue along a narrow enclosed path
to hop over a stile to a road.

Cross the road and go over the stile
ahead then keep ahead across a field,
passing to the left of two large oak trees
and, at the field edge, by a public

footpath signpost, turn right, **F** .

The path curves left and passes a stile
to reach a bridleway where you turn
left, through a hedge gap and head
diagonally right to the corner of the
field. Bear left along a track and at the
T-junction by Southbrook Farmhouse,
turn right along a gravel bridleway
and follow this as it veers to the right
and crosses a stream before reaching
the A25.

Turn left to go under the railway
bridge and return to where the walk
began.   ●

Effingham Forest and Netley Heath

Effingham Forest and Netley Heath

		GPS waypoints
Start	West Hanger car park	✍ TQ 070 493
Distance	9½ miles (15.2km)	Ⓐ TQ 076 496
Height gain	820 feet (250m)	Ⓑ TQ 079 504
Approximate time	4½ hours	Ⓒ TQ 084 505
Parking	West Hanger car park, Staple Lane, East Clandon	Ⓓ TQ 089 507
		Ⓔ TQ 120 499
Route terrain	Enclosed paths, woodland tracks	Ⓕ TQ 113 487
		Ⓖ TQ 077 489
Ordnance Survey maps	Landrangers 186 (Aldershot & Guildford) and 187 (Dorking & Reigate), Explorers 145 (Guildford & Farnham) and 146 (Dorking, Boxhill & Reigate)	

Much of this walk is through woodland and after passing some farms the path ascends gradually to a very steep descent through the trees. The outward route is along a pretty valley and the return, along the North Downs Way with good views of the Surrey countryside.

✍ From the West Hanger car park in Staple Lane cross the road and keep ahead at the North Downs Way signpost to enter the edge of woodland, with a field to your left. At the road turn left along it, and after a little over ¼ mile turn left just before the road curves right at a bridleway sign Ⓐ.

The path initially runs beside a wire fence and later becomes enclosed between fields before eventually joining a gravel lane at Woodcote Lodge. Keep ahead between farmhouses and bear left at a fork Ⓑ along a gently ascending path past stables. Keep along the bridleway and turn right at a fence along a farm track, to a lane. Turn right here and the lane descends around a sharp right-hand bend. To the left are now views of Effingham Forest. At a bridleway sign turn left Ⓒ and at a

fork, bear left again to a road. Turn left and just past a house on the left turn right at a bridleway signpost Ⓓ and then head uphill passing to the right of Mountain Wood.

Keep ahead as the woodland path descends steeply to reach a track. Cross over, pass a metal gate and continue along the byway on the edge of Effingham Forest. Go under horseshoe-shaped Troy Bridge, one of two that cross Sheepwalk Lane and built in the 1860s by the Earl of Lovelace for horsedrawn vehicles. The earl, a Victorian entrepreneur, who was educated at Eton was also a keen forester and architect who married Ada, Lord Byron's daughter. He built around 15 bridges, of which ten remain, to make timber removal easier. The Lovelace Bridges Project now maintains the Grade II-listed bridges.

Continue along this woodland path and eventually, after passing under the second bridge, you will pass to the left of a farmhouse. At a T-junction by a metal gate bear left and keep ahead at a path junction, to reach a lane. Cross the lane and continue along the byway to a metal barrier just before another road. Turn right **E**, at a public footpath sign into woodland, bearing left to cross another bridleway and continue along a wide track with woodland either side. The path enters the woodland of White Downs and then narrows and joins the North Downs Way by an information board – notice the steep escarpment on your left here. You should follow the acorn signs denoting the North Downs Way now, passing through a gate, then

North Downs Way view

bearing right to go through a kissing-gate and later passing to the left of a couple of pillboxes, relics from the Second World War which were part of London's outer defences. Just after a Greensand Way sign the path curves right to a road **F**.

Cross the road and bear right to continue along the North Downs Way which weaves its way through trees to White Down Lease. Go through a gate to enter this area of rare chalk grassland. The path passes more pillboxes and then ascends and becomes wide and grassy. Go through a kissing-gate and cross a track, one of the old drove roads once used for moving cattle. Go through another kissing-gate to enter an area called Blatchford Down and after two more kissing-gates, turn left. Pass a viewpoint at a gap in the trees and keep straight ahead at a main path crossing to enter Netley Heath. This area of Ice Age acidic soil was

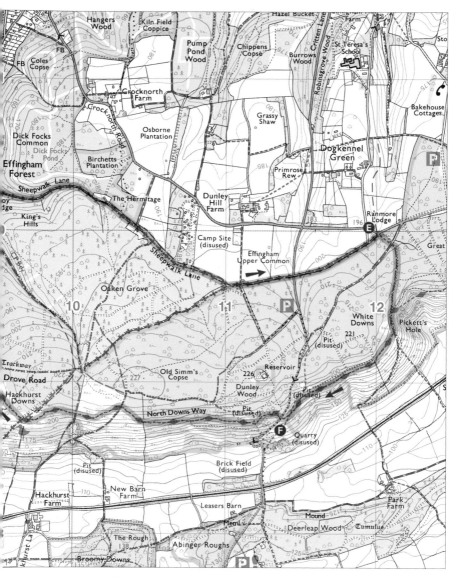

where thousands of Canadian troops were billeted during the Second World War as the allies prepared for the Normandy landings in 1944 and self-sown pine and conifer plantations have reclaimed much of it, although you'll also see birch and oak.

Ignore side paths and at a path junction in front of a Netley Plantation sign, cross the track and pass beside a metal barrier **G**.

At some farm buildings bear right at a path junction and keep along the wide track, bearing right at a fork. Over to the left are the woodlands of West Hanger and Combe Bottom which both contain some Neolithic flint quarries.

At a lane turn right and a few paces farther turn left at the North Downs Way sign to return to West Hanger car park. ●

Shere and Hurt Wood

Start	Reynards Hill, Winterfold Heath		**GPS waypoints**
Distance	9½ miles (15.2km)		TQ 074 425
Height gain	985 feet (300m)		**Ⓐ** TQ 082 423
Approximate time	4½ hours		**Ⓑ** TQ 085 430
Parking	Car park no. 4, Reynards Hill, Winterfold Heath		**Ⓒ** TQ 083 445
			Ⓓ TQ 083 465
			Ⓔ TQ 084 475
Route terrain	Bridleways, woodland paths, two pretty villages		**Ⓕ** TQ 068 478
			Ⓖ TQ 065 449
Ordnance Survey maps	Landrangers 186 (Aldershot & Guildford) and 187 (Dorking & Reigate), Explorer 145 (Guildford and Farnham)		**Ⓗ** TQ 073 435

A long and exhilarating walk beginning with a climb to the top of Pitch Hill before following a path through Hurt Wood to Peaslake, a village in the Greensand Hills, and then heading to the beautiful village of Shere. There are some steep climbs and a walk along a deeply rutted lane.

With your back to the car park turn right to the T-junction and cross the road to the public footpath sign 'Greensand Way'. Follow the waymarkers, turning right alongside the fence to

Bridleway on the edge of Winterfold Wood

Four Winds house, down to reach the road beside Mill Cottage. Cross the road and turn right to continue along the Greensand Way as it climbs past a quarry pit to the triangulation pillar at the top of Pitch Hill **Ⓐ**.

The views from here are among the

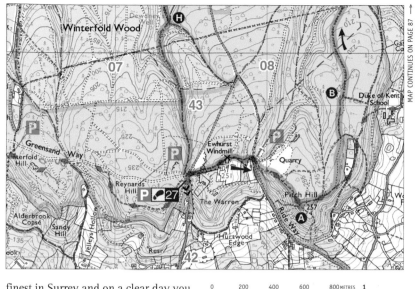

MAP CONTINUES ON PAGE 87

finest in Surrey and on a clear day you can see over the Weald of Surrey as far as the English Channel.

Follow the Greensand Way as it runs beside wooden hand rails and then as it broadens among the trees. At the next waymarked post, instead of turning right downhill, keep ahead leaving the Greensand Way to reach a broad crossway **B**.

Keep ahead along this wide, sandy bridleway and follow it through Hurt Wood, bearing left to descend at a fork.

With more than 60 miles of access tracks the Hurt Wood on the Greensand Ridge is the largest area of commonland in Surrey. In 1926 it was one of the first privately owned areas in the country to adopt a 'right to roam' and features a great many Scots Pine trees, planted here in the 18th century.

At a T-junction turn right and continue past a car park (no. 2) to the road. Turn right **C**, and follow the roadside path on the right as it ascends to a tarmac road. Bear left, passing to the right of Peaslake church and at the road turn right and then left at the **Hurtwood Inn** into Pond Lane. At the fork with Burchetts Hollow go through

the kissing-gate opposite, beside a public footpath sign, and cross the field to Jesses Lane. Turn right, at the next T-junction turn left, and after 100 yds turn right into Birches Lane **D**. Continue along the waymarked footpath to the left as it initially passes houses and later becomes enclosed. After the path curves right, turn left to join a bridleway. Keep ahead along this leafy tunnel to a road and pass under a railway bridge.

Turn left **E**, along High View and at the road junction, cross over and continue along Gravelpits Lane. At the fork beside Gravelpits Farmhouse turn right along the bridleway and over to the right is Netley Park. Soon the spire of Shere church comes into view ahead. Where the enclosed path ends continue across the right-hand field edge and at a path junction turn right to pass beside the church and a row of shops to a road. Opposite is the **White Horse** pub and to the left, **The William Bray**.

Shere is a popular location for filming and the church and adjacent

Triangulation pillar at the top of Pitch Hill

row of shops were featured in the pilot episode of the TV series, *Foyle's War*.

Turn right and just before the bridge turn left and follow a path beside the Tilling Bourne stream that passes a row of cottages and the tidy village allotments before curving right.

Cross the wooden footbridge beside the ford and keep ahead to continue along 'The Foxway' footpath to the right of The Old Rectory.

At the lane turn left **F**, and cross Chantry footbridge over the Tilling Bourne. Keep ahead along a shady bridleway that runs to the left of a garden fence. At a fork with a central waymarker, turn right and look out for where you turn left 40 yds farther, along an uphill bridleway through Shere Heath. Cross a road and at a T-junction turn left and go over the

railway crossing with care. Turn right and follow the track (Ponds Lane), which is sometimes deeply rutted, for about 1½ miles.

Just after the path passes the entrance to Lockhurst Hatch Farm turn left at a bridleway sign along a narrow track **G**.

At a fork bear left past a house and follow the blue waymarkers along this delightful, leafy bridleway. At the next waymarked fork turn right and continue along the valley of Winterfold Wood.

Much of this is privately owned and part of the Hurt Wood area of the North Downs. Apparently, some of the proceeds of the Great Train robbery were also buried here. At the 4-way path junction turn right **H**.

Cross a track, bear left at the next fork and maintain direction steadily uphill to return to the car park at the start of the walk. ●

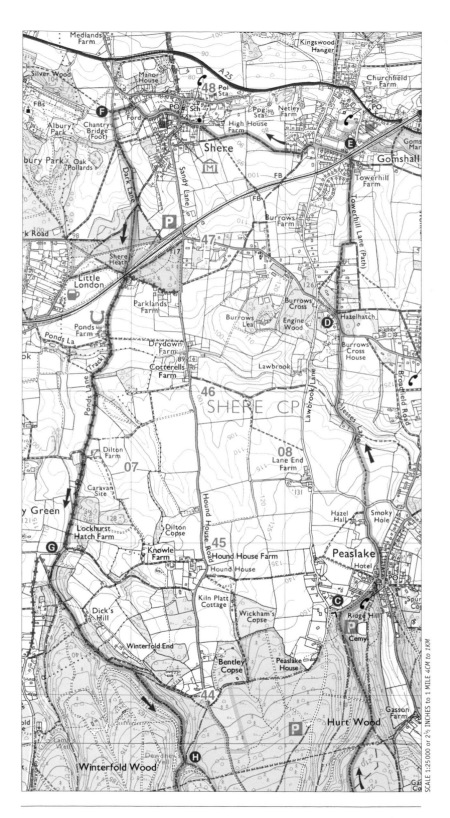

SCALE 1:25 000 or 2½ INCHES to 1 MILE 4CM to 1KM

Box Hill

		GPS waypoints
Start	National Trust Information Centre, Box Hill	�B TQ 179 513
Distance	11 miles (17.7km)	Ⓐ TQ 179 511
		Ⓑ TQ 172 513
Height gain	1,720 feet (525m)	Ⓒ TQ 158 512
Approximate time	5½ hours	Ⓓ TQ 139 504
Parking	National Trust car park, Box Hill	Ⓔ TQ 140 515
		Ⓕ TQ 147 542
Route terrain	Woodland paths, some steep climbs and descents	Ⓖ TQ 161 538
		Ⓗ TQ 170 533
Ordnance Survey maps	Landranger 187 (Dorking & Reigate), Explorer 146 (Dorking, Box Hill & Reigate)	Ⓙ TQ 178 532
		Ⓚ TQ 184 516

The greater part of this route is through woodland that is recovering well from the hurricane of 1987. It is advisable to pack a picnic and to take mud-proof footwear, unless the weather has been unusually dry. In the final section of the walk, after Mickleham, there are some quite demanding climbs.

Walk with your back to the National Trust Information Centre at Fort Cottages, which take their name from a stronghold and ammunition store built here in the late 19th century, and turn right to the viewpoint and triangulation pillar Ⓐ. The view southwards is spectacular, with the ground dropping away almost sheer to the River Mole some 400ft below. Descend to the right of the viewpoint and turn right onto the footpath and at a yellow North Downs Way waymarker turn left down steps.

At a waymarked post turn left to go steeply downhill through a group of yews. Steps have been cut into this path. Soon the River Mole can be glimpsed below, and you will see a signpost giving the choice of crossing the river either by stepping stones Ⓑ or footbridge. The former method, bearing left, is more fun and offers the shorter route. Go up the track on the other side to the main road –

the path from the footbridge rejoins here.

Take great care in crossing the dual carriageway. There is a track almost directly opposite which passes below the railway and then into the Denbies Wine estate. This vineyard covers much of the side of the valley to the east of Ranmore.

Several footpaths cross the track, but keep on the North Downs Way after it curves south for about 200 yds, then at a signposted crossing of tracks Ⓒ turn right along a bridleway off the North Downs Way into Ashcombe Wood. After another 200 yds uphill, a footpath sign directs you to the left and further uphill.

The path continues steadily uphill through woods, latter flattens out and becomes a metalled, then concrete road passing Denbies Farm. There may be deer in enclosures on your left. Pass straight on through a gateway to the public highway.

Carry straight on along the quiet lane to reach Ranmore. A bridleway runs along the wide verge, where walking is easier than on tarmac. Pass the Victorian flint church at Ranmore, bear right at the main road – the bridleway is now on the right – and pass the National Trust car park on the left. Immediately after the three houses on the right (the third, called Fox Cottages, has pantiles and tall chimneys) there is a track with a sign to the youth hostel ❶.

A few paces farther, bear left at a fork. This is a lovely stretch of a mile or so of woodland walking and then the roof and chimneys of Polesden Lacey can be seen over a clearing to the left. The house becomes hidden as the track drops down to the picturesque youth hostel, Tanner's Hatch ❷, where a bridleway joins from the left.

Pass the hostel and continue downhill along a delightful track which reaches the bottom of an open valley, and keep ahead at a fork by a blue waymarked post in the Connicut Lane direction. Walk along the track to pass beneath a balustraded bridge carrying an estate road over the track. The climb is steep for a while through Freehold Wood.

Turn right onto Polesden Road, where there is a parallel bridleway on the left. Where Polesden Road meets another road, cross straight over to walk up a track with paddocks to the left. This track, known as Admiral's Road, skirts Great Bookham and once it has crossed another bridleway it becomes a field edge path, narrow and enclosed for a short distance before meeting a track into Norbury Park.

Turn right onto this track ❸ and go down the hill to pass Roaringhouse Farm. Keep straight on after the red brick farmhouse up a bridleway which climbs steeply to start with and then descends abruptly. Keep straight ahead when a track crosses the bridleway and continue up through a group of yew trees. The bridleway meets another track at a blue waymarker. Bear left and walk along the track a short way to another junction with

View from Box Hill

a picnic site, an information board about Norbury Park and a signpost. Keep ahead with fencing to your right.

The bridleway passes the drive to Norbury Park house, the home of Dr Marie Stopes at the time of her death in 1957. The bridleway joins the drive from the house, before leaving it to the right. Pass another entrance to the house and bear right, keeping beside the fencing. The route follows the perimeter fence to a signpost on the right to a viewpoint ❹. It is worth the short detour to visit this spot where a seat has been placed so that the fine view southwards to Box Hill may be enjoyed in comfort. The viewpoint must be one of the few good things to have followed the 1987 hurricane, which opened up the vista.

Returning to the bridleway, this descends steeply to reach a surfaced track. Remain on the track until it swings sharply to the left. Keep straight on here on a narrow path. Turn right when the track meets a lane at the bottom, to cross a bridge over the River Mole to the main road. Take care when crossing this to the road opposite, which leads to Mickleham.

Turn left immediately past the church onto a driveway to Eastfield Cottage ❺. At a gate take the footpath over the stile to the right. This path through the woods soon begins to climb. Bear right at a fork

and note the remains of a wall of dressed flint on the right. Go straight over Mickleham Downs Road. At the top of the following climb, the path swings to the right and begins to descend through a grove of yews. In the middle of these it swings right again **J** and then suddenly the view opens up ahead. There is a seat here. The path then begins a slippery descent to Juniper Bottom, or Happy Valley. Although steps have been cut for the latter

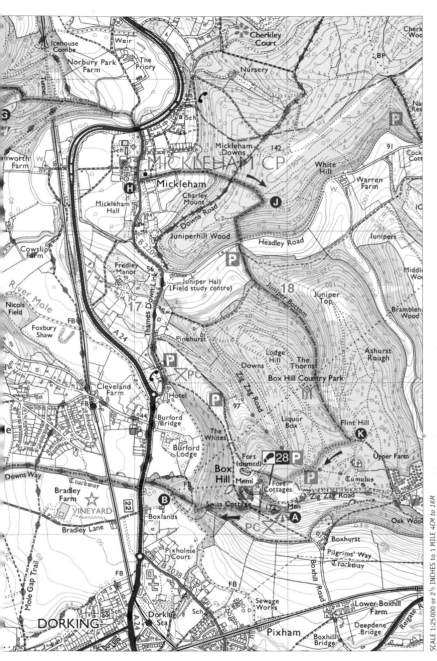

part of the way, great care has to be taken initially, especially after wet weather. Cross the road at the bottom to enter Juniper Bottom.

The final part of the walk is through a valley flanked by rich woodland that gradually encroaches on the track as it climbs. Posts with numbers denote stages of a National Trust nature trail. Almost at the top of Juniper Bottom, at post 14 **K**, turn right to leave the bridleway. Level walking follows through the woods; you may see deer. At a clearing bear right back to the car park. ●

SCALE 1:25000 or 2½ INCHES to 1 MILE 4CM to 1KM

Further Information

Walking Safety

Although the reasonably gentle countryside that is the subject of this book offers no real dangers to walkers at any time of the year, it is still advisable to take sensible precautions and follow certain well-tried guidelines.

Always take with you both warm and waterproof clothing and sufficient food and drink. Wear suitable footwear, such as strong walking boots or shoes that give a good grip over stony ground, on slippery slopes and in muddy conditions. Try to obtain a local weather forecast and bear it in mind before you start. Do not be afraid to abandon your proposed route and return to your starting point in the event of a sudden and unexpected deterioration in the weather.

All the walks described in this book will be safe to do, given due care and respect, even during the winter. Indeed, a crisp, fine winter day often provides perfect walking conditions, with firm ground underfoot and a clarity unique to this time of the year. The most difficult hazard likely to be encountered is mud, especially when walking along woodland and field paths, farm tracks and bridleways – the latter in particular can often get churned up by cyclists and horses. In summer, an additional difficulty may be narrow and overgrown paths, particularly along the edges of cultivated fields. Neither should constitute a major problem provided that the appropriate footwear is worn.

The Ramblers' Association

No organisation works more actively to protect and extend the rights and interests of walkers in the countryside than the Ramblers' Association. Its aims are clear: to foster a greater knowledge, love and care of the countryside; to assist in the protection and enhancement of public rights of way and areas of natural beauty; to work for greater public access to the countryside; and to encourage more people to take up rambling as a healthy, recreational leisure activity.

It was founded in 1935 and then Ramblers' Association has played a key role in preserving and developing the national footpath network, supporting the creation of national parks and encouraging the designation and waymarking of long-distance routes.

Our freedom of access to the countryside, now enshrined in legislation, is still in its early years and requires constant vigilance. But over and above this there will always be the problem of footpaths being illegally obstructed, disappearing through lack of use, or being extinguished by housing or road construction.

It is to meet such problems and dangers that the Ramblers' Association exists and represents the interests of all walkers. The address to write to for information on the Ramblers' Association and how to become a member is given on page 95.

Walkers and the Law

The Countryside and Rights of Way Act (CRoW Act 2000) extends the rights of access previously enjoyed by walkers in England and Wales. Implementation of these rights began on 19 September 2004. The Act amends existing legislation and for the first time provides access on foot to certain types of land – defined as mountain, moor, heath, down and registered common land.

Where You Can Go
Rights of Way
Prior to the introduction of the CRoW Act, walkers could only legally access the countryside along public rights of way. These are either 'footpaths' (for walkers only) or 'bridleways' (for walkers, riders on horseback and pedal cyclists). A third category called 'Byways open to all traffic'

Countryside Access Charter

Your rights of way are:

- public footpaths – on foot only. Sometimes waymarked in yellow
- bridle-ways – on foot, horseback and pedal cycle. Sometimes waymarked in blue
- byways (usually old roads), most 'roads used as public paths' and, of course, public roads – all traffic has the right of way

Use maps, signs and waymarks to check rights of way. Ordnance Survey Explorer and Landranger maps show most public rights of way

On rights of way you can:

- take a pram, pushchair or wheelchair if practicable
- take a dog (on a lead or under close control)
- take a short route round an illegal obstruction or remove it sufficiently to get past

You have a right to go for recreation to:

- public parks and open spaces – on foot
- most commons near older towns and cities – on foot and sometimes on horseback
- private land where the owner has a formal agreement with the local authority

In addition you can use the following by local or established custom or consent, but ask for advice if you are unsure:

- many areas of open country, such as moorland, fell and coastal areas, especially those in the care of the National Trust, and some commons
- some woods and forests, especially those owned by the Forestry Commission
- country parks and picnic sites
- most beaches
- canal towpaths
- some private paths and tracks Consent sometimes extends to horse-riding and cycling

For your information:

- county councils and London boroughs maintain and record rights of way, and register commons
- obstructions, dangerous animals, harassment and misleading signs on rights of way are illegal and you should report them to the county council
- paths across fields can be ploughed, but must normally be reinstated within two weeks
- landowners can require you to leave land to which you have no right of access
- motor vehicles are normally permitted only on roads, byways and some 'roads used as public paths'

(BOATs), is used by motorised vehicles as well as those using non-mechanised transport. Mainly they are green lanes, farm and estate roads, although occasionally they will be found crossing mountainous area.

Rights of way are marked on Ordnance Survey maps. Look for the green broken lines on the Explorer maps, or the red dashed lines on Landranger maps.

The term 'right of way' means exactly what it says. It gives a right of passage over what, for the most part, is private land. Under pre-CRoW legislation walkers were required to keep to the line of the right of way and not stray onto land on either side. If you did inadvertently wander off the right of way, either because of faulty map reading or because the route was not clearly indicated on the ground, you were technically trespassing.

Local authorities have a legal obligation to ensure that rights of way are kept clear and free of obstruction, and are signposted where they leave metalled roads. The duty of local authorities to install signposts extends to the placing of signs along a path or way, but only where the authority considers it necessary to have a signpost or waymark to assist persons unfamiliar with the locality.

The New Access Rights
Access Land

As well as being able to walk on existing rights of way, under the new legislation you now have access to large areas of open land. You can of course continue to use rights of way footpaths to cross this land, but the main difference is that you can now lawfully leave the path and wander at will, but only in areas designated as access land.

Where to Walk

Areas now covered by the new access rights – Access Land – are shown on Ordnance Survey Explorer maps bearing the access land symbol on the front cover.

'Access Land' is shown on Ordnance Survey maps by a light yellow tint surrounded by a pale orange border. New orange coloured 'i' symbols on the maps will show the location of permanent access information boards installed by the access authorities.

Restrictions

The right to walk on access land may lawfully be restricted by landowners. Landowners can, for any reason, restrict access for up to 28 days in any year. They cannot however close the land:

- on bank holidays;
- for more than four Saturdays and Sundays in a year;
- on any Saturday from 1 June to 11 August; or
- on any Sunday from 1 June to the end of September.

They have to provide local authorities with five working days' notice before the date of closure unless the land involved is an area of less than five hectares or the closure is for less than four hours. In these cases landowners only need to provide two hours' notice.

Whatever restrictions are put into place on access land they have no effect on existing rights of way, and you can continue to walk on them.

Dogs

Dogs can be taken on access land, but must be kept on leads of two metres or less between 1 March and 31 July, and at all times where they are near livestock. In addition landowners may impose a ban on all dogs from fields where lambing takes place for up to six weeks in any year. Dogs may be banned from moorland used for grouse shooting and breeding for up to five years.

In the main, walkers following the routes in this book will continue to follow existing rights of way, but a knowledge and understanding of the law as it affects walkers, plus the ability to distinguish access land marked on the maps, will enable anyone who wishes to depart from paths that cross access land either to take a shortcut, to enjoy a view or to explore.

General Obstructions

Obstructions can sometimes cause a problem on a walk and the most common of these is where the path across a field has been ploughed over. It is legal for a farmer to plough up a path provided that it is restored within two weeks. This does not always happen and you are faced with the dilemma of following the line of the path, even if this means treading on crops, or walking round the edge of the field. Although the later course of action seems the most sensible, it does mean that you would be trespassing.

Other obstructions can vary from overhanging vegetation to wire fences across the path, locked gates or even a cattle feeder on the path.

Use common sense. If you can get round the obstruction without causing damage, do so. Otherwise only remove as much of the obstruction as is necessary to secure passage.

If the right of way is blocked and cannot be followed, there is a long-standing view that in such circumstances there is a right to deviate, but this cannot wholly be relied on. Although it is accepted in law that highways (and that includes rights of way) are for the public service, and if the usual track is impassable, it is for the general good that people should be entitled to pass into another line. However, this should not be taken as indicating a right to deviate whenever a way becomes impassable. If in doubt, retreat.

Report obstructions to the local authority and/or The Ramblers.

Useful Organisations

Campaign to Protect Rural England
CPRE National Office
128 Southwark St, London SE1 0SW
Tel. 020 7981 2800
www.cpre.org.uk

Forestry Commission
Great Eastern House, Tenison Road,
Cambridge CB1 2DU
Tel. 01223 314546
www.forestry.gov.uk

Forest Enterprise
South East England Forest District
Bucks Horn Oak, Farnham Surrey GU10 4LS
Tel. 01420 23666

Long Distance Walkers' Association
www.ldwa.org.uk

North Downs Way
www.nationaltrail.co.uk/northdowns

Surrey Hills
www.surreyhills.org

The National Trust
PO Box 39, Warrington WA5 7WD
Tel. 0844 800 1895
Regional office for the south east
Polesden Lacey, Dorking
Surrey RH5 6BD
Tel. 01372 453401

Natural England
Victoria House, London Square,
Cross Lanes, Guildford, GU1 1UJ
Tel. 0300 060 2620
www.naturalengland.org.uk

Ordnance Survey
Romsey Road, Southampton SO16 4GU
Tel. 08456 05 05 05
www.ordnancesurvey.co.uk

Ramblers' Association
2nd Floor Camelford House,
87-90 Albert Embankment
London SE1 7TW, UK
Tel. 020-7339 8500
www.ramblers.org.uk

Youth Hostels Association
Trevelyan House,
Dimple Road,
Matlock, Derbyshire,
DE4 3YH
Tel. 01629 592600
www.yha.org.uk

Tourist Information Centres
Elmbridge: 01372 474474
Epsom: 01372 432000
Guildford: 01483 505050
Mole Valley: 01306 879327
Reigate & Banstead: 01737 276000
Runnymede: 01932 838383
Surrey Heath: 01276 707100
Tandridge: 01883 722000
Waverley: 01483 523333
Woking: 01483 755855

Ordnance Survey maps of Surrey

Surrey is covered by Ordnance Survey
1:50 000 scale (1$\frac{1}{4}$ inches to 1 mile or 2cm
to 1km) Landranger map sheets 175, 186
and 187. These all-purpose maps are packed
with information to help you explore the
area. Viewpoints, picnic sites, places of
interest and caravan and camping sites are
shown, as well as public rights of way
information such as footpaths and bridleways. To examine Surrey in more detail,
and especially if you are planning walks,
Ordnance Survey Explorer maps at
1:25 000 (2$\frac{1}{2}$ inches to 1 mile or 4cm to
1km) are ideal:

133   Haslemere & Petersfield
134   Crawley & Horsham
145   Guilford & Farnham
146   Dorking, Box Hill & Reigate
147   Sevenoaks & Tonbridge
160   Windsor, Weybridge & Bracknell

To get to Surrey, use the Ordnance
Survey Travel Map-Route Great Britain at
1:625 000 (1 inch to 10 miles or 4cm to
25km) scale.

Ordnance Survey maps and guides
are available from most booksellers,
stationers and newsagents.